S0-BAC-040

Catawba Royale . . .
Cranberry-Scented Sparkling
Apple Cider . . . Not-So-Bloody
Mary Slush . . . White Grape Juice
Sangria . . . Banana and Orange
Smoothy . . . Lime & Mint Julep . . .
Hot Chocolate Milk . . . Real
Ginger Ale . . . Cranberry/Cherry
Punch Bowl . . .

You'll find easy-to-make recipes for these and many other exotic and great-tasting concoctions in this comprehensive bartender's guide for the teetotaler. Here are recipes for hot and cold drinks, after-workout boosters, New Year's sparklers, soda fountain specials, tropical fruit coolers, flavored ice cubes, fruit and vegetable garnishes, and much, much more. This classic collection of drink recipes will help you create the perfect alcohol-free taste sensation every time!

MARIE SIMMONS is the author of the best-selling *365 Ways to Cook Pasta* and the co-author with Lori Longbotham of the forthcoming *Better by Microwave*. A former senior editor at *Cuisine* and contributing editor to *Good Food*, Simmons is the co-author of a monthly column in *Bon Appétit* with Richard Sax. She lives in Brooklyn and Sag Harbor with her husband and their teen-age daughter.

BARBARA J. LAGOWSKI is a freelance writer and editor with a special interest in cookbooks.

THE BARTENDER'S GUIDE TO ALCOHOL-FREE DRINKS

by
Marie Simmons
and
Barbara J. Lagowski

(Originally titled *Good Spirits*)

A SIGNET BOOK

A Word of Thanks
To Elizabeth Rozin, whose *Flavor-Principle Cookbook*
inspired our formulation of the flavor principle
used in creating the drinks in this book.

SIGNET
Published by the Penguin Group
Penguin Books USA Inc., 375 Hudson Street,
New York, New York 10014, U.S.A.
Penguin Books Ltd, 27 Wrights Lane,
London W8 5TZ, England
Penguin Books Australia Ltd, Ringwood,
Victoria, Australia
Penguin Books Canada Ltd, 2801 John Street,
Markham, Ontario, Canada L3R 1B4
Penguin Books (N.Z.) Ltd, 182–190 Wairau Road,
Auckland 10, New Zealand

Penguin Books Ltd, Registered Offices:
Harmondsworth, Middlesex, England

Published by Signet, an imprint of New American Library, a division
of Penguin Books USA, Inc. This book appeared previously under
the title *Good Spirits* in a Plume edition.

First Signet Printing, November, 1990
10 9 8 7 6 5 4 3 2 1

Contents

A New Style of Drinking and Entertaining

A toast to high sobriety and to the kind of festive spirits that simply can't be poured from a bottle! People coast to coast are raising their glasses to their own well-being and to a style of social drinking that emphasizes the flow of lively conversation rather than the flow of alcohol. They've sampled the wide variety of sophisticated bottled waters now available, and their demand for heady tastes without the heaviness of alcohol has made the "mocktail" and alcohol-free "wine" a must on the menus of many restaurants—from neighborhood pubs to the finest eating establishments.

And now, at last, here is the mixing guide that enables you to drink to the alcohol-free life-style in the most intimate, appropriate setting of all—your own home. Celebrate all of your special occasions, whether a romantic Valentine's Day à deux, a rousing Octoberfest, or a warm, welcoming open-house to ring in the holiday season, with a variety of flavorful alcohol-free libations that will give your guests an occasion they can —and *will*—remember.

Here's Looking at You

Good friends and good times—these are the mixers that special events are truly made of. But how does the blend differ when alcohol, long believed to be an ice

7

breaker and a social lubricant, is not an integral part of your recipe for a good party?

Professional caterers and bartenders agree—if you want your guests to stay longer, to mix more freely, and to get beyond the polite small talk, make your next get-together alcohol-free! Unspiked delights keep energy levels high and minds sharp, encouraging movement, mingling, and meaningful conversation. So celebrate those people who add a special kick to your life by mixing up a convivial cup that stimulates rather than dulls the senses, that energizes rather than depletes the mind and body. And don't be surprised if they—and your party—last well beyond the stroke of midnight.

To Your Health

Drinks without alcohol are blends of pure ingredients —flavorful, healthful meldings of fresh flavors and textures, free of the heavy "bite" that numbs the senses as well as the taste buds. Drinks without alcohol are also drinks without ethanol, a depressant much like ether. (Now you know why that slow and steady alcohol-induced inertia is known as "getting stiff!") Ethanol, the active ingredient in all alcoholic drinks, clouds the mind, slows the reflexes, and dulls perception while flooding the body with empty carbohydrate calories, ultimately ushering in that fuzzy, headachy period known as the morning after. The result? A party you barely remember followed by a day you'd rather forget.

Celebrate the alcohol-free life-style and both you and your guests will feel better for it before, during, and *after* the last snifter or punch cup is put away. The nonalcoholic kick is a flavor kick that stimulates the appetite for good food and lively conversation. Sample our Catawba Royal or our White Grape Juice Sangria and you'll wake up energized, alert, ready to raise your glass again to the health and well-being of those special people who add spirit to all the occasions of your life.

And a special note to those who work out or get their highs from sports: while all of our recipes, from the sophisticated spritzers to the exotic quenchers, are bursting with flavor as well as vitamins, you'll want to lift a few of our energy-powered bracers (page 76) to recharge after your exercise program. These après-workout revivers are specially formulated to deliciously nourish and replenish the body you've trimmed and toned, *without* adding excess calories.

Skoal! Prosit! A Taste of the Melting Pot

Fill your glasses with the lushest treasures of the world—heady, exotic flavors and the richest of textures —and your taste buds will demand that you drink them "straight!" Whether you choose to quench the heat of your best curry with a creamy rosewater-spiked Indian lassi or warm up a poolside crowd with tropical coolers, the most unusual taste sensations are no farther away than your favorite market or health food shop.

Complement your favorite ethnic dishes with exotic alcohol-free potables to savor the unique and subtle tastes of the world to the fullest. Or intoxicate your senses by sampling these spirited international delights at an around-the-world-in-one-evening tasting party. But whether you choose the kiwi or passion fruit of the tropics, the "dry" varietal grape juices coaxed from the finest grapes, or the aromatic herbs and spices of the East, a cornucopia of exciting new tastes is within your reach.

A Toast to Your Creativity!

Is there a secret to the perfectly balanced nonalcoholic drink? You bet there is, and we're going to share it with you. Once you plug your own favorite taste sensations into our "flavor principle," you'll soon be blending, mixing, and shaking up the kind of punchy beverages sure to shake up any crowd. You'll find your own creativity will be the key ingredient in mixing up elegant, energizing alcohol-free nips and coolers that are as limitless as your imagination.

9

So start to celebrate the times of your life *now*—with elegant slushes, stylish spritzers, and very adult coolers —all alcohol-free. And be merry—the "proof" of truly festive spirits was *never* an alcohol content.

Stocking the Alcohol-Free Bar

The effervescent spritzers, hearty warmers, and sophisticated coolers that ring in the special events of your life are as unique as your guests, as diverse in spirit as the holidays and festive occasions you celebrate, and as exotic as the many countries that make up the world of taste sensations. Serving them in anything but the appropriate glasses, without a taste-enhancing garnish or a flavorful ice would steal a bit of the luster from your gala. Take the time to present these elegant punches, zingers, and ales in a festive way—garnished, iced, and sparkling—and you'll bring out the best in these unique libations, your guests, and your party.

RAISING THE RIGHT GLASSES

The best glassware for the colorful, flavorful, alcohol-free drinks you'll be stirring, mixing, and shaking is *clear* glassware. The lush, sherbety hues of tropical coolers are meant to be seen; the savory vegetable blends are a feast for the eyes as well as the taste buds. The potency of these heady concoctions is in their freshness. Let your guests drink it in with all of their senses.

The glasses on the following pages have sizes and shapes that will show off the drinks in this book to best advantage. Some can do double duty for more than one type of beverage.

10- to 14-Ounce Tumbler or Tall Glass: A showcase for iced coffees, teas, tall coolers, summertime fizzes, and splashy spritzers. Also apropos for long fruit drinks, from purees to nectar blends.

8- to 10-Ounce Rocks Glass: Fill your "lowballer" with savory specialties made to be served over ice, from spicy vegetable crushes to light-but-lively aperitifs. For added elegance, choose rocks glasses with short, stubby stems.

8-Ounce Oversized Martini Glass: Broad at the rim, tapered at the stem, this is the best choice for ices, slushes, and frozen delights. Reach for it when mixing up elegant oversized "mocktails," as well.

8- to 10-Ounce All-Purpose Wine Glass: As versatile as they make them! A large balloon stem elegantly accommodates anything from tall slushes to alcohol-free fizzes to blends based on the latest "dry" wines. A *must* to make the most of aromatic drinks.

6- to 8-Ounce Champagne Tulip: For a bit of the bubbly (alcohol-free, of course!). Capture the effervescence of sophisticated sparkling drinks in a tulip. A champagne flute glass can also be used. An elegant glass for elegant drinks.

6- to 8-Ounce Punch Cup: Planning drinks for a crowd? Pre-chill these handy, inexpensive sippers, supply a bowl of cheer, then relax. Your guests will serve themselves.

8- to 10-Ounce Heatproof Glass, Mug, or Cup: For warming fall and winter delights, mulled ciders, spiced coffees, and bracing teas. Preheat by rinsing with hot water.

FLAVORED ICE CUBES AND ICE RINGS

If you really want to warm up your celebration, head for the freezer. The sound of ice against glass is a signal that it's time to relax, to enjoy good times and good friends, and to share a welcoming glass of something wholesome, fresh, and delicious. But ice doesn't have to be just a chiller for your alcohol-free delights. Use our special fruit-and-vegetable-base ice cubes to enhance the flavor of a punch or add some kick to the already-potent natural flavors of healthful refreshers. Our flavored cubes and rings won't dilute your drink—they'll add a little something special.

Cubes as a Frozen Garnish

Fill a freezer tray with water and add to each section a fruit or vegetable embellishment appropriate to the drink you will be serving. For sweet drinks, try ripe strawberries, a bit of lemon zest, or a small wedge of fresh pineapple. When serving a spicy or savory drink, add a strip of bright green or red pepper, pearl onions, or if you can get fresh herbs, lemon-scented thyme, a bit of basil, or a few sprigs of mint. (Try growing a variety of herbs in your garden or on a sunny windowsill.)

Cubes for Double the Flavor

Chill your drinks with ice cubes made of the same delicious recipes that fill your glasses and double the flavor-power of your favorite libations. Just freeze two cups of juice instead of water in an ice cube tray until

13

solid, then remove to a plastic bag where you can keep the cubes on hand in your freezer. Feel free to give most blends of natural ingredients the big chill but *do* eliminate any carbonated mixers. Freezing will only flatten their flavor impact. For added kick, toss in a frozen garnish, as well.

Cubes for Cold Compatibility

Ice down your drinks with cubes of frozen flavor that are compatible with their main ingredients for a powerful melding of taste sensations. Liven the robust flavor of a savory drink with a cube of cucumber puree revved up with a dash of hot pepper sauce; lift the spirits of iced tea by pouring it over cubes of zesty orange, lemon, or lime ice. Or chill your tropical favorites with frozen peach or honeydew puree and a hint of mint, then wait for the delicious meltdown.

Cubes made of the frozen recipe itself or of a compatibly flavored ice can be crushed, by hand or in a blender, to lend a pebbly consistency to the finished drink. You can also blend or whirl the cubes in a food processor until they become a slush, mound the ice in the center of a broad-rimmed cocktail glass, and pour the drink around it. Garnish, and you've created a cool, refreshing island of flavor.

Molded Rings to Ice the Punch Bowl

To cool off a summer punch for a crowd, nothing is more attractive or more practical than an ice mold composed of ice cubes, fruit juice, and pieces of fruit arranged decoratively. Here's how to do it:

Select a ring mold, preferably aluminum or plastic. Place a layer of ice cubes in the bottom of the mold, then arrange fruit on top of the ice, heaping and aligning as tightly as possible. (Try three colors of grapes—red, green, and purple—for a winter holiday punch. Wedges of apple—green Granny Smith and Golden or Red Delicious, skin side up—or slices of orange, lemon, or lime, cut nearly all the way across and twisted into an "S" to resemble bright flowers are also dazzlers!)

Fill the mold carefully with the juice that forms the basis of your punch. Then carefully transfer to a level spot in the freezer and freeze until solid.

To remove the ice ring from the mold, hold the mold under slowly running cool water for a few seconds to loosen the ice, then invert onto a plate. Transfer, fruit side up, to the punch bowl.

FRUIT AND
VEGETABLE GARNISHES

The most successful garnishes repeat and therefore reinforce a flavor in the drink (for instance, garnishing a fruit-flavored cooler with a slice of the fruit from which it was made). But just as often, a garnish adds a flavor element important to the balance of the drink (see "The Flavor Principle," page 149) or a compatible enhancement. A neutrally flavored ginger ale might be garnished with a slice of sweet/sour carambola (star fruit) or with kiwi to add some interest. But whether you intend the garnish to double the impact of the drink or act as an enhancement, it should be as attractive as it is flavorful.

Herbal or Leafy Garnishes

If an herb such as dill, mint, or basil is used to flavor a drink, try to use a sprig of the fresh herb. An herbal garnish (like that used in our Thyme-Scented Tomato Tonic Cooler, page 121) not only flavors the drink but adds an aromatic lift that also reinforces the taste.

Vegetable Garnishes

Many vegetables make excellent trimmers and swizzlers for savory drinks. Here are some of our favorites:

Carrots: Sticks and curls are both useful. To make

curls (great for hanging over the edge of a tall glass), use large carrots with a nice, fat core. Using a swivel-bladed vegetable peeler, pull the blade lengthwise down the carrot in even strokes, working from the fat end to the thin. (Press hard.) To set the curls, place in a bowl of ice water and refrigerate a few hours or overnight. Use any leftover pieces of carrot for carrot stick swizzlers.

Celery: Use the inside ribs from the heart of the stalk, and be sure to leave leafy tops intact.

Scallions: Trim away the outer layer, along with any uneven or broken tops, and cut the roots from the bulb. Especially good in tomato-based drinks but nice in carrot juice and other savory blends as well.

Jicama: A brown-skinned bulbous root with a very crunchy, white flesh that has recently become very popular. A neutral flavor but a barrel of texture, it is used in Mexican cuisine (often paired with orange sections and red onion in a salad). Pare and cut into ¼-inch-thick sticks 1 inch taller than the glass.

Fennel: A stalk vegetable that looks a little like celery but has a fat bulb on the bottom, wonderful fernlike tops and an addictive anise flavor. Garnish glasses with the outside ribs of this vegetable and guests will wonder which is better—the drink or the swizzler.

Cucumber: Choose small cukes, preferably ones that have not been waxed. (Waxed cucumbers must be peeled.) Cut into spears and scrape out the larger seeds or cut into ¼-inch slices, slit from center to edge, and hang on the rim of a glass. Provides great texture with a cooling effect.

Green and red bell peppers: Wedges work best in shorter rocks glasses.

Cocktail onions: A treat to find on the bottom of a savory vegetable cooler.

Pickled jalapeño peppers: Float on the surface of a tomato-based drink. (See Chili Pepper-Spiked Hot Tomato Juice, page 140.)

Fruit Garnishes

To make lush additions to fruit-based refreshers. Again, some of our favorites:

Strawberries: Keep stems attached, then slit the base of the berry and hang on the rim of a glass.

Citrus slices: Cut slices at least ¼ inch thick so that they are sturdy enough to stand upright without flopping over. To flute, "stripe" skin of whole fruit with a zester. Slit slices from center to edge and hang on the rim of a glass. Citrus slices can also be twisted into flowery shapes that are perfect for freezing in a floating ice mold (see page 14).

Fruit spears: Melons—cantaloupe, honeydew, watermelon—and sturdier fruits like papaya and pineapple can be cut into spears or wedges to use as a garnish. Remove the skin and seeds first unless you're using watermelon—you'll want to keep that green, speckled rind.

Kiwi: One of the prettiest fruits around. As a garnish, it can be peeled or not, sliced, slit from the center to the edge, and hung on the rim of a glass.

Whole berries: Fresh raspberries, blueberries, and strawberries, hulled and sliced, make an attractive garnish when just a few are floated on the surface of a drink. (Odd numbers are more interesting.)

Carambola: Also called Chinese star fruit (when you slice it, you'll see why!). Pale yellow, sweet, and slightly firm-textured. Star fruit is now available in some supermarkets and in many specialty produce stores.

Lemon or orange zest: Pare the skin of clean fruit with a zester or vegetable peeler, cutting away just the colored surface. (Avoid the white pith, which can be bitter.)

Shopping for Ingredients

HIDDEN TREASURES ON YOUR
SUPERMARKET SHELVES

While putting together this collection of recipes, we discovered and rediscovered not only the obvious drink ingredients but other products not normally associated with sipping under the guise of socializing. These ingredients, both the obvious and the not-so-obvious, are grouped here as you might find them in the supermarket aisles. By no means an exhaustive listing, this guide includes ingredients we've experimented with plus others which may inspire you to do some experimentation of your own.

Dairy

Check the refrigerated dairy cases for these drink bases and enhancers:
low-fat yogurt (all flavors)
buttermilk
milk, half and half, and heavy cream
cottage cheese and ricotta (blend smoothly)
sour cream
Refrigerated fruit drinks: apple, pear, or cherry cider; orange and grapefruit drinks. Iced tea (check your health food store for iced herbal blends); lemonade and orangeade.

Canned Fruits and Juices

To cut sweetness and heaviness, look for fruits canned in their own juices or light syrup.

Ask any grocer and he'll tell you that the juice shelves are expanding *fast*. Look for pure fruit juices rather than the combination fruit drinks, which tend to be high on sugar and low on definitive fruit flavor.

Grape: Pure grape juice was once relegated to one small corner. Not anymore! Grape juice is one of the most adult juices around, flavorful and light with a nice, dry finish. And now many of those grape varieties introduced to us by the California wine industry boom are showing up as varietal grape juices like White Zinfandel, French Colombard, and Chenin Blanc, to name a few. The result? A dazzling array of sophisticated, nonalcoholic "vintages," sparkling and still, white and delicate rosé, just perfect for elegant at-home entertaining. These juices, once hidden away in specialty food shops, are now appearing on supermarket shelves where they belong. Look for them—and for a new white juice, a powerful blend of apple, pear, and grape.

Apple: Available filtered and unfiltered, sweetened or pure and natural. Try one of the many sparkling nonalcoholic ciders for a festive and delicious treat.

Cranberry and its blended relatives: For the most distinctive cranberry flavor, choose the plain, unblended juice. Also try the unsweetened cranberry concentrate available in many health food stores; a sweetened variety can be found in supermarkets.

Exotic or tropical juices: These are often available as blends. Most popular and readily available flavors are papaya, mango, guava, and passion fruit. They give flavor, texture, and natural sweetness to drinks.

Vegetable juices: Sample the range of vegetable juices and blends, including the various tomato/clam and tomato/beef combinations. Carrot juice is another must-try, though do seek out fresh juice rather than canned for a real taste experience.

Teas and Coffees

The variety of teas, tea blends, herb teas, and flavored brews is overwhelming—but inspirational for nonalcoholic mixologists. Use them to create your own unique blends—and don't overlook the variety of coffees available either. Dark roasts, espresso roasts, spiced coffees, even flavored coffees (do sample the hazelnut if it's available in your area!) have expanded coffee options tenfold. Whether you ice them or drink them hot, the potential for experimentation is enormous.

Chocolate

Dutch-process cocoa is among the richest and most flavorful powdered chocolate products available on your supermarket shelves. Do opt for it when featuring chocolate-flavored drinks. Unsweetened and semisweet blocks are often used to provide a chocolate base for drinks. Chocolate-flavored syrups are best in soda fountain treats.

Freezer Case Products

Concentrated juices: Look beyond the usual array of frozen juices and you will find a little gem called tangerine juice concentrate. Light, sweet, with an uninhibited flavor, it may find a permanent place in your freezer.

Fruits: Stock up on the ten-ounce packages of quick-thaw fruits in light syrup and you'll always have drink bases conveniently at hand. The bags of loose-pack fruits are also useful, especially when fruit is not plentiful, and can be measured out cup for cup as a substitute for fresh fruits. Their quality is usually acceptable.

Frozen yogurts, sorbets, ices, ice cream: Of course. But go easy—many of these can make what was a refreshing drink into a dessert. The frozen yogurts are appealing because they deliver the treat without the fat and are not as creamy or "desserty" as traditional ice creams.

Flavored Sodas

For a look at the sparkling waters, club sodas, and seltzers that add a bit of the bubbly to your drinks, see page 26. As for flavored sodas, which have the potential to be a truly great drink base, look beyond the mundane. Some uniquely flavored (even naturally flavored) sodas offer a great deal of kick as well as intense taste, so do experiment. An exciting jump-off point would be ginger beer, a hot, assertive, and bubblingly satisfying drink just right for adult palates. You may also want to try the alcohol-free beers available in this section, or the mixers like tonic, Tom Collins mix, or bitter lemon, all geared for the adult palate.

Fresh Produce

Always look for fruits and vegetables that are at their height of ripeness, or plan ahead and buy still-hard fruits, then ripen them at home in a brown paper bag. If you are planning to use the skin of the fruit, be sure to wash it very well—this is especially true when you're planning to use the zest of dimpled citrus fruits. Melons make an especially good drink base. Strawberries, raspberries, peaches, nectarines, apricots, pears, apples, bananas, pineapples, and figs are wonderful additions to blended concoctions. Exotic fruits like kiwi (which are becoming more widely available and less exotic every day), mango, papaya, passion fruit, fresh dates, and carambola (star fruit) add a touch of the tropics to your potables and are a must for creative exploration.

Dried Fruits

A wonderful way to sweeten hot and cold drinks naturally when sugar is not a welcome sweetener. Pitted prunes, dried figs, apricots, apples, dates, even raisins, can be added to blended drinks to sweeten and add texture and fiber.

Other Sweeteners

Sugar: Opt for superfine when you can find it. This bartender's standard melts away almost instantly without ever leaving drinks with that grainy texture that undissolved granulated sugar can impart.

Jams, honeys, and marmalades: All of these products dissolve quickly and flavor exotically. (See our recipe for Marmalade Tea, page 40, as an example.)

Artificial Sweeteners: Substitute for sugar using the ratio found in the package directions.

Herbs

Fresh herbs are powerful additions to drinks. Basil and dill team successfully with tomato. Basil and orange is a favorite combination, as is thyme with orange or lemon. To enhance a lime or tomato drink, try coriander (cilantro). One way to team herbs with other flavors is to try to make associations with foods you have eaten and enjoyed. A memorable pasta dish served in a light tomato sauce that had been enhanced with some finely grated orange zest served as the inspiration for our flavorful Tomato and Orange Cooler (see page 98).

Remember to use dried herbs sparingly—they are concentrated and a little goes a long way.

Spices

Use your cherished flavor associations to spice your holiday drinks as well. For fall and winter drinks, use cinnamon, allspice, nutmeg, mace, and ginger with apples and cranberries. Use freshly ground pepper as a counterpoint accent to add interest to vegetable-based drinks.

Specialty Items

When mixing your own, experiment with some of these unique and flavorful specialty products. If they are not available locally, you can find them through mail order catalogs for kitchenware and gourmet food products.

Stem ginger in syrup
Raspberry and other concentrated fruit syrups
Orange slices and pineapple spears in light syrups
Coffee-flavored syrup
Canned cream of coconut
Tropical fruit syrups (usually available in West Indian or Spanish markets).

TREASURES FROM FARMERS' MARKETS AND PRODUCE STANDS

The ciders from farmers' markets are not only the freshest but are available in imaginative flavors, like pear, cherry, strawberry, as well as the ubiquitous apple. Interesting varieties of white and purple grape juices are often available in grape-producing areas. You can count on these farm stands to make available the freshest produce known to man (unless you can pick produce from your own garden). Strawberries are often picked at their ripest and sold that same day; the tomatoes have never been subjected to the adversity of a refrigerator.

ETHNIC FOOD STORES

Ethnic specialty shops are often an excellent source for unusual or hard-to-find items. Browse through Greek or Arabic stores for wonderfully rich and tangy plain yogurt, dark roasted coffee, and freshly ground herbs and spices. Oriental groceries are an excellent source for traditional teas. Indian markets carry good-quality canned mango, both whole and pureed, and also offer long cinnamon sticks, and other spices such as cardamom, curry, and coriander. Italian markets are a source of excellent coffees, fruit-flavored syrups, and imported sparkling waters. Polish groceries are known for their high-quality canned fruits, preserves, and fruit syrups. Exotic fruit juices and fruit-flavored syrups are also available in Spanish or Puerto Rican markets as well.

These bustling neighborhood markets are a veritable treasure trove of unique ingredients and new culinary experiences. Experiment and you'll learn that food is the true universal language.

HEALTH FOOD STORES

Fresh Juices

For garden-fresh fruit and vegetable juices, take advantage of your health food store's juice bar. Many of the freshly extracted juices you'll find there—like carrot and celery juice—far surpass canned varieties in flavor. And all fresh juices abound in vitamins and minerals.

Herbal Teas

Health food stores offer a wealth of herbal teas in hundreds of imaginative flavor combinations. A worthwhile area of exploration particularly for those who prefer their hot or iced teas without caffeine.

Juice Concentrates

Pure extracted juice with no additives but plenty of flavor.

Whole-Milk Yogurts

Look for unique flavors such as maple and vanilla with honey.

Sweeteners

Health food stores offer sweet alternatives for those who would rather keep refined white sugar out of their drinks.

Honeys

Try natural honeys for distinctively flavored sweeteners. Clover will be light and delicate; alfalfa honey rich and mellow.

Dried Fruits

Healthy, flavorful alternatives to processed sugars and honeys. Dried fruits in the supermarket may have been processed with sulfur dioxide—and may contain preservatives. Count on health food stores for sun-dried apricots, dates, figs, and prunes, all packaged without additives.

Jams and Jellies

Check health food shops for sugarless jams, jellies, and preserves which can be used to flavor and sweeten hot teas. (See our Marmalade Tea, page 40.)

Wheat Germ

For added protein and B vitamins, blend wheat germ into your energy-powered drinks. Available either roasted or raw.

Fresh Seasonings

Ginger root, naturally grown peppers, fresh herbs, all are available to you as part of the health food bounty. Experiment with these organically grown flavor-enhancers and you'll add a spicy kick to all your alcohol-free potables.

Bottled Juices

A plethora of flavors from exotic passion fruit to sparkling nonalcoholic grape juice and apple cider. An excellent source for the relatively new varietal grape juices, such as Chenin Blanc or French Colombard. Also some interesting and unusual flavors like Blueberry Nectar, Strawberry-Raspberry, and Coconut-Pineapple.

Also, be sure to check the shelves of your health food store for an array of sparkling waters, nuts, tofu, and other soy-based products. The recommended shopping list here is nearly endless.

BOTTLED WATERS—CHOOSING MIXERS AND EXTENDERS

"Welcome to the water generation," hailed *Time* magazine. "People order their eau by brand name, as they once did their Scotch." In the United States, bottled water has become the fastest growing beverage as consumers continue to join the movement to drink less and enjoy it more.

The array of available flavors and types of bottled waters can be daunting. For those bottled-water aficionados whose thirst simply cannot keep up with the constantly surging tide of product, we offer this short course on the sparkling and mineral waters that are now overtaking the supermarket shelves.

Pure, Still Waters

These are generally marketed as "spring waters." These noncarbonated eaux can, for the most part, be considered to be free of pollutants, chlorine, and additives. Because they do not sparkle, most are consumed as simple thirst quenchers or table waters.

Mineral Waters

Whether naturally carbonated or still, these waters draw certain mineral properties from the rock strata of their geographic region which may be considered beneficial to health. These minerals account not only for their "curative" reputation but for their vast differences in taste. (Some can be quite hearty.) These waters are tested for purity, filtered, and stripped of any iron content, but with these exceptions, are bottled nearly straight from the source.

Naturally Carbonated Waters

These get their bubbles from naturally formed carbon dioxide, although this gas may be drawn off in the bottling process and then reintroduced to keep the levels of sparkle constant.

Commercially Carbonated Sparkling Waters

This category includes seltzers, club sodas, and tonics which get their fizz courtesy of commercial bottlers. After filtration and chilling, carbon dioxide is pumped into the waters at a very high level of pressure. Seltzers often are sodium free, devoid of sugar, and contain no preservatives at all. Their distinctively clear appearance, slightly bitter taste, and robust effervescence make them a natural extender for nearly any kind of blended drink. Club sodas are often flavored with a hint of salt, and tonics are lip-pursing "dry" extenders, distinctively flavored for truly adult appeal.

In many of our recipes, we call for seltzer water. Please understand that we are using the term *almost* generically to mean a sparkling extender. If you prefer to substitute club soda or your favorite sparkling mineral water, please feel free to experiment.

And do dip into the array of flavored, non-sweet, effervescent waters now available at most markets. Zipped up, with the essences of orange, lemon, lime, grapefruit, and other popular fruits, these waters were made for adding sparkle and a hint of flavor to your drinks. But first, a few guidelines:

- Generally, citrus flavors are compatible and interchangeable. Just remember that orange is fuller flavored and "feels" sweeter. Lemon and lime are more citrusy-bitter.
- Because citrus is acid/bitter in taste, it is a perfect accompaniment for fruits that are sweet/acid in flavor. For instance, adding a squirt of lemon or lime to a naturally sweet apple juice would enhance the nearly nectar-like juice. But if you were to team a sweet apple flavor with orange, you would probably still need a shot of acid (lime or lemon straight) to balance the sweetness.

This point is applicable to the use of fruit-flavored seltzers and sparkling waters as well. A sweeter juice should be balanced by an acidic carbonated water. If your drink is a blend of two sweet fruit juices, then a very acidic citrusy-water would be the best extender. (See "The Flavor Principle," page 149, for an in-depth discussion of balancing flavors.)

Spirited Celebrations
for Every Occasion

Let the good times roll! The reasons to eat, drink, and be merry are as diverse as each new day, as unique as the people who make those celebrations so special. Toast to those warm and festive family holidays, the special events like weddings, birthdays, anniversaries, the happy camaraderie of an impromptu tailgate party or even a classic can't-miss movie on the VCR—and wash those good feelings down with the kind of robust chill-chasers and refreshers that won't dilute or distort the spirit of the occasion.

People's drinking habits have changed for the better, and now, with this book, so have alcohol-free drinks. For the first time ever, high-sobriety celebrations take on a truly *adult* twist, with the snappy tastes and sophisticated textures that tickle the mature palate.

So bottom's up—savor those red-letter days with the healthy, wholesome, grown-up bracers guaranteed to keep those good times rolling.

NEW YEAR'S SPARKLERS

Gather your dearest "aulde" acquaintances; welcome your more recently acquired kindred spirits; then count off the hours before midnight with festive rounds of the liveliest, most elegant sparkling sippers ever lifted in honor of old Father Time.

There is no place like home for an intimate celebration of the memories you've made and a toast to the good things yet to come. Dress up your party space with streamers, splash multicolored confetti on cocktail and occasional tables, set out a sumptuous assortment of elegant hors d'oeuvres —then top off your finest crystal flutes or tulip glasses with these lushly colored, sophisticated blends of tart "dry" wines, ripe fruit, and a touch of seltzer water.

An elegant, colorful dazzler.

Catawba Royale

1 teaspoon raspberry syrup *
6 ounces sparkling Catawba white grape
   juice, well chilled **
Thin curl of orange zest

Spoon raspberry syrup into a champagne glass. Slowly add the chilled sparkling grape juice. Twist the orange zest to release the fragrant oils and drape over the rim and into the glass.

This drink looks very much like a Kir Royale (the classic champagne and cassis cocktail of France), and evokes the same elegant aura.

YIELD: 1 6-ounce serving.

SERVE WITH: Cheese straws and open-faced smoked salmon sandwiches on toast.

* Imported from Europe and available in 17-ounce bottles in ethnic or specialty food stores.
** One bottle (750 ml./25.4 fluid ounces) of grape juice will yield approximately 4 6-ounce drinks.

A cider with a tangy kick.

Cranberry-Scented Sparkling Apple Cider

1 teaspoon unsweetened cranberry concentrate *
6 ounces sparkling apple cider, well chilled **
Lime slices

Spoon cranberry concentrate into an all-purpose wine glass. Slowly fill the glass with well-chilled cider. Garnish with a lime slice, slit and set on the rim of the glass.

The pucker-power of the cranberry concentrate is a perfect balance for the slightly sweet overtones of the sparkling cider. The result? A truly elegant drink that rivals any aperitif.

YIELD: 1 6-ounce serving.

SERVE WITH: Something salty like an assortment of olives, shrimp dipped in mustard mayonnaise, or pumpernickel bread spread with cream cheese and topped with salmon caviar.

* Cranberry concentrate is available in health food stores in 8-ounce bottles (enough for 48 6-ounce drinks).
** One bottle (750 ml./25.4 fluid ounces) of sparkling cider is adequate for 3 6-ounce drinks.

Peach and Ginger Spritzer

⅓ cup peach puree *
1 tablespoon ginger syrup (see page 113)
   or syrup from jar of stemmed ginger in
   syrup
Seltzer water, well chilled
Lime slice

Place peach puree in a champagne glass, add ginger syrup, then slowly top with cold seltzer water. Garnish with a lime slice.

YIELD: 1 8-ounce serving.

SERVE WITH: A platter of sliced prosciutto and thinly sliced dried salami; pass pretty baskets of bread sticks and crackers.

* To make peach puree, thaw a 10-ounce package of frozen peaches in light syrup according to package directions. Puree in a food processor or blender. This is adequate for 4 8-ounce drinks.

Tangerine Sparkle

**1 tablespoon tangerine juice concentrate,
   thawed ***
Seltzer water, well chilled *
Fresh strawberries

Place tangerine juice concentrate in a flute or tulip glass. Slowly add the seltzer water. Garnish by slitting the base of a strawberry and hooking it onto the rim of the glass.

YIELD: 1 6-ounce serving.

SERVE WITH: Thin slices of smoked turkey breast arranged on slices of dark pumpernickel bread, thinly spread with chutney, and more whole strawberries with a creamy, fresh chèvre to spread on the berries.

* A 6-ounce can of tangerine concentrate and 2½ quarts of seltzer water are enough for 12 6-ounce drinks.

APRÈS SKI
Warm Drinks
for Cold Hands

When the boots stamp at the doorstep, when the last sodden mittens are hung by the hearth to dry, you'll want to cozy up to the kind of hearty drinks that chase the chill from your bones, relax those tired muscles, and prepare you for a long, lazy evening spent stoking the fire. Count on these warmer-uppers to rekindle your energies for another day in the lift lines.

A good, old-fashioned chill-chaser.

Hot Lemonade

2 tablespoons sugar
1 lemon
8 ounces boiling water

Place sugar in a mug. Cut the lemon in half; cut off a thin slice of lemon; remove seeds from slice and place in mug.

Squeeze the juice from the lemon halves (3 to 4 tablespoons) into the mug. Add the boiling water; stir to dissolve the sugar.

YIELD: 1 8-ounce serving.

SERVE WITH: Slices of toasted and buttered banana bread, toasted English muffin slathered with grape jelly, or a wedge of moist carrot cake.

Hot Curried Tomato Juice

1 tablespoon butter
1 tablespoon curry powder
1 quart tomato juice
¼ cup plain yogurt
Ground cumin

Heat the butter in a saucepan until melted. Stir in the curry powder; sauté in butter over low heat until fragrant, about 30 seconds.

Add the tomato juice to the saucepan; heat to simmering. Ladle into 4 mugs. Top with a dollop of yogurt and sprinkle lightly with ground cumin.

YIELD: 4 8-ounce servings, or 1 quart.

SERVE WITH: Cubes of sharp Cheddar cheese and raw crudités such as green bell pepper strips, cucumber spears, and carrot sticks.

*A steaming bracer for
weak skier's knees.*

Hot Spiced Pineapple
and Lemon "Tea"

1 cup water
1 cup pineapple juice
4 whole cloves
1 lemon
1 tablespoon sugar

In a saucepan, slowly heat the water and pineapple juice with 2 cloves until boiling.

Cut the lemon in half; cut off one slice and cut slice in half crosswise and set aside. Stick a clove into white pith of each piece of lemon. Squeeze the juice from lemon halves and combine with the sugar, stirring together until dissolved.

Off heat, gradually stir the lemon and sugar mixture into the boiling pineapple mixture. Pour into 2 mugs; float a half of a lemon slice in each mug.

YIELD: 2 8-ounce servings.

SERVE WITH: Unsalted, roasted cashews, Brazil nuts, and pecans.

*An irresistible
melding of two favorites.*

Mocha Mugs

⅓ cup unsweetened cocoa powder
½ cup sugar
2 cups hot brewed coffee (or 1 tablespoon
   instant plus 2 cups hot water, or to
   taste)
2 cups milk
½ teaspoon pure vanilla extract
½ cup heavy cream
Ground cinnamon

Stir the cocoa and sugar together in a saucepan. Gradually stir in the coffee. Add the milk.

Heat, stirring frequently, until simmering. Remove from heat. Stir in the vanilla.

Whip the cream until thickened. Ladle the chocolate mixture into 4 mugs. Float a spoonful of cream on each. Sprinkle with cinnamon.

YIELD: 4 8-ounce servings, or 1 quart.

SERVE WITH: Chocolate-covered graham crackers—and don't forget to dunk!

*Marmalade is reputed to have been created in
honor of Mary Queen of Scots.
When added to hot, brisk tea,
it makes for a zesty pickup.*

Marmalade Tea

Boiling water
Teabags
Orange marmalade

Brew a pot or a mug of strong tea (see How
to Brew a Pot of Tea, page 91). Add marmalade to
taste (about 2 rounded teaspoonsful per 8 ounces
of tea) and stir until dissolved. Be sure to savor the
bits of bittersweet orange rind in between sips.

SERVE WITH: Molasses cookies.

*Delivers a double-barreled
flavor/energy impact.*

Hot Double Apple Punch

½ cup packed, dried apple slices
1 cup water
1 quart apple juice
6 allspice berries
3 whole cloves
4 cinnamon sticks

Combine the apple slices and water in a large saucepan; heat to simmering. Cover and let stand off heat for 10 minutes.

Add the apple juice, allspice, and cloves. Heat to boiling; cover and simmer for 10 minutes.

Ladle into 4 mugs, distributing the apple pieces evenly. Add a cinnamon swizzler to each serving.

YIELD: 4 8-ounce servings, or 1 quart.

SERVE WITH: Warm apple turnovers or pumpkin cheesecake.

*A sweet way to warm up
from the inside out.*

Hot Spiced Apricot Nectar

1½ quarts apricot nectar*
**2 tablespoons mixed mulling spices, tied
in a piece of cheesecloth****
1 lemon
1 orange
Cinnamon sticks

Heat the nectar and mulling spices in a large saucepan to boiling; cover and simmer over low heat for 15 minutes. Let steep, covered, off heat, for 1 hour.

Remove the bag of mulling spices. Reheat the nectar to simmering. Remove from heat.

Cut the lemon and orange in half. Slice 1 half of each thinly; remove the seeds. Squeeze the juice from the remaining halves. Add the slices and juice to the nectar.

Ladle into 6 mugs. Garnish each with a cinnamon stick swizzler.

YIELD: 6 8-ounce mugs, or 1½ quarts.

SERVE WITH: Ripe pears, Gorgonzola cheese, and walnuts in their shells.

---

* For an interesting variation, try half apricot nectar and half cranberry juice or look for a bottled cranberry-apricot combination.
** Available loose or already tied into cheesecloth pouches. Assemble your own by mixing 1 cinnamon stick, crushed, 1 teaspoon of whole cloves, a couple of pieces of dried ginger, 6 allspice berries, and a grating of fresh nutmeg.

Ratna Kolhatkar, a food enthusiast and fine teacher of food science, taught us how to prepare this favorite Indian-style tea.

Aromatic Cardamom Tea

4 cups cold water
4 whole cardamom pods, crushed with
back of spoon
4 heaping teaspoonfuls Darjeeling tea
Sugar, to taste
Hot milk or cream, to taste

In a small saucepan, combine the water and cardamom. Heat slowly over low heat until boiling. Meanwhile, rinse a teapot with very hot water and add the tea leaves.

Pour the cardamom-infused water over the tea leaves. Cover and let steep for 3 to 4 minutes. Cover with a kitchen towel or a tea cozy to keep warm. Pour through a tea strainer into cups. Pass the sugar and milk and add to taste.

YIELD: 4 servings.

SERVE WITH: Warm currant scones or raisin-bran muffins and sweet butter.

SUNDAY BRUNCH

You've only been away from the grind for twenty-four short hours. Yet, with the morning paper settled comfortably on your lap and the buttery fragrance of flaky croissants wafting through the house, work couldn't seem further away. The doorbell rings—and soon your friends are sharing the simple pleasures of breathing in the deep, rich aroma of freshly ground coffee, relaxing with the magazine section, and savoring that first tall, savory eye-opener of the day.

At its best, brunch is a long, leisurely awakening of the body, the mind, and the senses. No bumps, no jolts—just an extended, enjoyable yawn of pleasure. When planning your brunch, try to center it in the most comfortable location you can. And whether you set this over-easy repast in your cozy country kitchen or on the terrace, remember: late-rising guests like to linger, cradling their warm mugs until the very last moment. So sink in—and bring those sleepy taste buds back to life with this rousing reveille of morning refreshers.

More gazpacho than Bloody Mary, this is the quintessential brunch drink gone to Spain and frozen into a lovely, smooth slush along the way. The key ingredient here is the tangy ice —tomato juice cubes spiked with horseradish and vegetables.

Not-So-Bloody-Mary Slush

1 quart tomato juice
¼ cup bottled horseradish or
    2 tablespoons freshly grated *
¼ cup each chopped green bell pepper,
    celery, and scallion, including the green
    top
Hot pepper sauce, to taste
4 inside ribs of celery with their leafy tops

In a blender or food processor, puree half of the tomato juice with the horseradish, green pepper, celery and scallion; add hot pepper sauce. Pour into an ice cube tray and freeze until solid. Place glasses in the freezer at least 1 hour before serving.

At serving time, empty cubes into food processor or blender. Add remaining tomato juice; process until smooth. Pour into frosted wine glasses. Garnish with celery rib swizzle sticks.

YIELD: 4 8-ounce servings, or 1 quart.

SERVE WITH: Avocado halves filled with shrimp salad or French bread with Brie.

* Depending on the potency of the fresh product.

*The bite of the unsweetened grapefruit juice
and the cool, herbaceous flavor of the
cucumber make this a powerful refresher.*

Grapefruit and Cucumber Cooler

3 well-chilled cucumbers
1 quart unsweetened grapefruit juice*
1 tablespoon sugar, or to taste (optional)
4 sprigs mint (optional)

Pare 2 of the cucumbers; quarter lengthwise. (If they are very large, scoop out the seeds—otherwise, leave them intact.) Cut the cucumbers into 1-inch chunks. (There should be about 1½ cups.)

Scrub the remaining cucumber, score with the tines of a fork. Cut into ¼-inch slices. Reserve for garnish.

Place the cucumber chunks and 2 cups of the grapefruit juice in the blender or processor. Puree.

Pour into a large pitcher. Add the remaining grapefruit juice. Taste. If it is too tangy, stir in 1 tablespoon of sugar until dissolved.

Pour into rocks glasses. Cut a slit in the reserved cucumber slices and set one on the rim of each glass; garnish with mint if desired.

YIELD: 4 8-ounce servings, or a generous quart.

SERVE WITH: Scrambled eggs and smoked salmon on toasted English muffins.

* The flavor of grapefruit juice made from concentrate and sold in bottles in the refrigerator section of the market is preferable to that of the canned variety.

A zesty, sparkling eye-opener.

White Grape Juice Sangria

1 orange
1 lemon
1 tray ice cubes, preferably orange- or
   lemon-flavored (see page 123)
28-ounce bottle white grape juice
32-ounce bottle seltzer water
1 lime, sliced

With a small, sharp knife, cut the zest from both the orange and the lemon in one long spiral, working from the top to the bottom of the fruit. Squeeze the juice from the orange and the lemon.

Place the ice cubes in a pitcher; add the grape juice, seltzer, orange and lemon juices. Add the spirals of orange and lemon zest. Stir with a large spoon.

Pour into wine glasses and garnish each with a lime slice.

YIELD: 8 8-ounce servings or 1 large pitcher, about 2 quarts.

SERVE WITH: A big bowl of ice-cold seedless green grapes, skillet corn bread, huevos rancheros, and orange and jicama salad.

Orange Mist

6 cups orange juice
2 tablespoons lime juice
2 cups ginger ale, well chilled
2 kiwi fruit, pared and cut into ¼-inch
slices

Pour 2 cups of the orange juice into an ice cube tray. Freeze until solid. Transfer to a plastic bag and have ready in the freezer.

At serving time, place half of the ice cubes in the blender. Add 2 cups of orange juice and 1 tablespoon of lime juice. Puree the mixture until slushy. Transfer to a glass pitcher.

Repeat with the remaining ice, orange juice, and lime juice. Transfer to a pitcher. Add the ginger ale; stir gently to blend.

Pour into wine glasses. Garnish each with a slice of kiwi, slit and hung on the rim of the glass.

YIELD: 8 8-ounce servings, or 1 large pitcher, about 2 quarts.

SERVE WITH: Challah bread French toast and sautéed apple slices.

*As bright and as beautiful
as a Caribbean sunrise.*

Tropical Coconut Punch

3 tablespoons cream of coconut *
1 cup mango and papaya juice, well
    chilled
1 teaspoon fresh lime juice
1 papaya, skin removed, halved, seeded,
    and cut into ½-inch wedges

Add cream of coconut, mango and papaya
juice, and fresh lime juice to the blender. Puree.**
   Pour into wine glasses and garnish each with a
piece of fresh papaya.

YIELD: 1 8-ounce serving.

SERVE WITH: Omelets filled with fruit preserves and
cream cheese (try strawberry, blueberry, or cantaloupe preserves).

* Cream of coconut is available in 15-ounce cans, enough for
10 drinks. (Any remaining cream of coconut can be scraped
into a plastic container, covered tightly, and refrigerated for
up to one week—or frozen for later use.)
** For an icy-cold drink, add about ¼ cup of cracked ice to
the blender for every 8 ounces of juice.

49

VALENTINE'S DAY
À DEUX

Turn the lights down low, but set out enough softly glowing candles so that you can feast your eyes on each other—and on these deliciously romantic, wildly potent love potions!

Whether you can walk your way to your lover's heart blindfolded or are still looking for some route markers, this is a night to celebrate the adventure of an amorous journey. Begin by making a warm, sensuously spicy menu your billet-doux: whet your appetites with ripe tomatoes (love apples) stuffed with crab meat salad, and stir the senses with a tender steak au poivre, crisp oven-roasted potatoes, and a salad you can share—two forks, one bowl.

Then fall in love all over again while savoring this special evening—and the kind of heady crushes, spritzers, and sweet teasers you can come to dote on.

*The perfect ending for
an intimate dinner for two.*

Iced Chocolate
Espresso Coffee

2 cups strong, fresh-brewed, hot espresso
   coffee
½ cup superfine granulated sugar
1 square (1 ounce) semisweet chocolate,
   chopped *
¼ cup heavy cream
Chocolate-covered coffee beans

Stir the hot coffee, sugar, and chocolate together until the sugar dissolves and the chocolate melts. Refrigerate until well chilled—3 hours, or overnight.

Fill wine glasses with finely crushed ice. Pour the cold coffee over the ice.

Whisk the cream until just thick enough to mound on a spoon. Place a spoonful on each glass. Top with a chocolate-covered coffee bean. Serve with a small spoon or a thin straw.

YIELD: 2 8-ounce servings.

SERVE WITH: The rest of the beans and a platter of chocolate truffles.

* Or use 1 ounce of bittersweet chocolate.

*It is red, it is zingy, and it is sweet as honey—
just the way to wrap up a
Valentine's Day repast.*

Honey Red Zinger Tea

**2 bags Red Zinger tea
2 tablespoons honey
2 lemon slices
2 whole cloves**

Place a tea bag in each of 2 clear glass mugs or tea cups; brew for 3 to 4 minutes. Remove the tea bags; add 1 tablespoon of honey to each mug.

Float a lemon slice studded with a clove in each mug.

YIELD: 2 cups.

SERVE WITH: Any cinnamon-spiced sugar-coated shortbread or cookies.

A sophisticated way to dally with that second great love of your life—chocolate!

Very Grown-Up Hot Chocolate

¼ cup imported Dutch process cocoa
¼ cup vanilla sugar (see below)
½ cup heavy cream
1½ cups boiling water

Stir the cocoa and sugar together in a small saucepan until blended. Stir in the heavy cream gradually to make a smooth mixture.

Gradually stir in the boiling water. Keep warm over low heat. At serving time, pour into mugs or your best china cups.

YIELD: 2 8-ounce servings.

SERVE WITH: Marrons Glacés, a lovely chestnut confection available in specialty food shops, or miniature éclairs.

Vanilla Sugar

Tuck a vanilla bean into a pint jar filled with granulated sugar. Cover tightly and store in a cupboard for at least 2 weeks. The vanilla bean will perfume the sugar subtly. Add more sugar as you use it and you'll never run out.

What to serve at a head-over-heels flirtation? Try this one.

Strawberry Crush

10-ounce package frozen strawberries in light syrup
Juice and zest of 1 orange
Orange-flavored seltzer water or sparkling water, chilled (6 ounces per serving)

With your hands, break up the pouch of solidly frozen fruit into large chunks. Place in a food processor or blender.

Remove the zest of the orange with a zester or a sharp vegetable parer in long strips; reserve. Squeeze the juice (there should be about ½ cup); add to the processor or blender.

Puree the frozen strawberries until smooth. Place 2 rounded measuring tablespoons of the mixture in the bottom of each champagne glass.* Slowly pour in 6 ounces of chilled seltzer or sparkling water per glass; stir to form a nice foamy "head." Drape a spiral of orange zest into and over the edge of each glass, but first twist the zest to release the fragrant oils.

YIELD: up to 8 8-ounce servings.

SERVE: After dinner with fresh strawberries or as an aperitif with papaya or melon wrapped in paper-thin slices of ham (try Smithfield or Westphalian).

* If you are not using all of the strawberry mixture, scrape into a plastic container, cover tightly, and freeze for future romantic moments.

The passion fruit or purple granadilla really has nothing to do with the passion of romance and everything to do with religious fervor. Spanish Jesuit missionaries in South America named the complex blossom of this fruit for the passion of Christ, after seeing in its shape the symbolism of the crucifixion and resurrection.

Passion Fruit Spritzer

⅔ glass well-chilled passion fruit juice *
Wedge of lime
⅓ glass well-chilled seltzer water
Thin slice of lime

Fill champagne glass about ⅔ full with passion fruit juice. Squeeze in the juice of the wedge of lime. Top the glass off with seltzer water. Garnish with a slice of lime.

YIELD: 1 6-ounce serving.

SERVE WITH: Asparagus spears cooked al dente and served at room temperature, dipped in crème fraîche or clarified butter laced with lemon juice and grated lemon zest.

* The pure juice of the passion fruit has a very intense sharp/ sweet flavor. In all likelihood, you will only be able to purchase a blend of juices—passion fruit and apple, guava, and perhaps pineapple. This will be fine, as passion fruit juice is very expensive, hard to find, and probably too intensely flavored for most palates. If you do find pure juice, sweeten it with a little chilled simple syrup (page 88) before using.

A PAINTING/
RENOVATION
PARTY

For truly innovative homesteaders, what's old is what's new! And they've pitched right in, rejuvenating classic Georgians, revitalizing stately Victorians, conditioning country cottages, and putting a coat of very modern polish on everything from the red South 40 barn to the loftiest ceilings of elegant nineteenth-century brownstones.

For these hardy and creative souls, sweat equity begins on the day of the painting or renovation party, an active, participatory, let-it-all-hang-loose gathering of good friends and curious neighbors that has all but replaced the traditional and more formal housewarming in many circles.

Guests at these barn-raisers find it impossible to hang onto their inhibitions and a paintbrush at the same time. (One renovation party hostess, who decided to eliminate one nonload-bearing wall, provided her guests with some very "heavy" party favors—sledgehammers!—and a smashing good time was had by all.)

So put that door you've taken off its hinges across two sawhorses and set up a refreshing drink buffet, letting your friends mix and match their own concoctions. Because these are all fruit-based drinks, they are fairly substantial and nourishing— a perfect break from the rigors of moving, stripping wallpaper, or staining woodwork.

Honeydew, Grapefruit, and Ginger Smoothy

1 wedge (about 12 ounces) ripe honeydew,
   seeded and cut up (about 1 cup)
1 cup grapefruit juice
1 tablespoon lemon juice
2 to 3 tablespoons ginger syrup (see page
   113) or syrup from jar of stemmed
   ginger in syrup
½ cup cracked ice

Combine all ingredients in a blender. Whirl until thoroughly blended. Pour into a tall glass.

YIELD: 1 12-ounce serving.

*The perfect reviver when your
get-up-and-go has gotten up and gone.*

Fruit Spritzer

**1 wedge (about 12 ounces) ripe honeydew,
   seeded and cut up (about 1 cup)
1 peach or nectarine *
½ cup orange juice
½ cup cracked ice
Seltzer water, well chilled**

Puree honeydew, peach, orange juice, and
ice in a blender. Fill 2 tall glasses three-quarters
full. Top off with seltzer water.

YIELD: 2 10-ounce servings.

* Wash nectarines, but do not peel. Cut into 1-inch chunks. If
peach skin is thin, wash well to remove fuzz and leave skin
intact. If peach skin is thick, peel before cutting up. When
these fruits are out of season, use 1 cup of frozen unsweetened sliced peaches.

Cranberry and Honeydew Spritzer

1 wedge honeydew melon (about 12
    ounces), seeded, and cut up (about
    1 cup)
1 cup cranberry juice, well chilled
1 tablespoon lime juice
½ cup cracked ice
Seltzer water (optional)

Combine the honeydew, cranberry juice, and
lime juice in a blender. Whirl until thoroughly
blended. Pour into a tall glass; top off with a splash
of seltzer water if you wish.

YIELD: 1 12-ounce serving.

This fruit blend can be inspirational—especially when trying to smooth the lumps out of wet wallpaper.

Mixed Fruit Smoothy

1 large, juicy nectarine or peach *
1 cup orange juice
1 tablespoon lime juice
½ cup cracked ice

Puree the nectarine or peach, orange juice, lime juice, and ice in a blender. Pour into a tall glass.

YIELD: 1 10-ounce serving.

* Wash nectarines but do not peel. Cut into 1-inch chunks. If peach skin is thin, wash well to remove fuzz and leave skin intact. If peach skin is thick, peel before cutting up. When these fruits are out of season, use 1 cup of frozen unsweetened sliced peaches.

Banana and Orange Smoothy

1 banana
1 cup orange juice or ½ cup each orange and grapefruit juices
½ cup crushed ice
1 tablespoon lemon juice

Puree the banana, orange juice or orange and grapefruit juices, ice, and lemon juice in a blender. Pour into a tall glass and enjoy.

YIELD: 1 10-ounce serving.

AN INTERNATIONAL TASTING

Armchair travel is one of life's most fascinating and least expensive delights. But do your exotic dreaming while sipping an equally exotic cooler and your reveries will become more deliciously real!

To double your pleasure, reserve plenty of space for some well-chosen "travel" companions. Fill your home with adventurous guests and explore the flavors of the world together. Whether you serve up a sizzling tandoori feast, complete with light, airy Indian breads, and top it off with a refreshing glass of savory saffron-laced lassi or end a lovely Italian repast with a rich, pudding-like La Cioccolata Goldoniana, the flavorful experience will be worth writing home about.

For larger crowds, an eclectic, international tasting party can be every bit as invigorating as touring around the world in just one evening! Mix up batches of refreshing Italian Frulati or Hot Spiced White Grape Glog, then surround these favorite national beverages with ethnic finger foods.

And no matter where you hang your hat (or store your suitcases), remember: Taste sensations from every corner of the world are no farther away than your local market. Drink them in!

Prosit!

The drink that energizes and cools nearly all of Italy during those warm summer months.

Frulati di Frutta (Fruit Whip)

1 cup fresh fruit, peeled, and if necessary, pitted *
⅔ cup milk
2 teaspoons sugar (optional, depending on sweetness of fruit)
¼ cup cracked ice

Combine all the ingredients in a blender. Blend for at least 1 minute, or until the ice is finely chopped or dissolved. Pour into a tall glass.

YIELD: 1 generous serving, about 2 cups.

* In Italy, where this drink is a popular sidewalk café libation as well as midmorning snack, some of the favored flavors are peach, strawberry, banana, and apricot. But when vendors offer tropical or exotic fruit frulati—made from kiwi, pineapple, mango, papaya, or cantaloupe—business really booms!

*Chocolate in the style of Goldoni, a 16th-
century Venetian playwright. Sinfully rich,
hopelessly addictive. This recipe is adapted
from an Italian cookbook,* Venetian Cooking
*by Giuseppe Maffioli and was translated
by Michele Scicolone.*

La Cioccolata Goldoniana

2 cups cold water
6 ounces semisweet or bittersweet
    chocolate, coarsely chopped
¼ cup sugar
1 tablespoon cornstarch
½ teaspoon vanilla extract
Pinch of cinnamon

In a heavy saucepan, combine the water and
chocolate. Stir the sugar and cornstarch together
in a small bowl to blend; add to the saucepan.

Heat the mixture, stirring constantly with a
whisk, until the chocolate melts and the mixture
boils and thickens.

Stir in the vanilla and cinnamon.

Pour into small espresso cups. Serve piping hot.

This chocolate is rich and thick, almost like
unset pudding. Serve it anytime—as they do in
Italy, or as we do—after dinner.

YIELD: 6 4-ounce servings, or 2½ cups.

*Savory or sweet, this nutritional cooler offers
a refreshing taste of exotic India.*

Lassi

Few strands saffron
2 tablespoons hot tap water
1 cup plain yogurt
2 tablespoons heavy cream (optional) *
2 tablespoons sugar
½ cup cold water
½ cup cracked ice

In a small bowl combine the saffron and hot tap water. Let stand for 10 minutes.

Combine the soaked saffron, yogurt, heavy cream, if using, sugar, cold water, and ice. Blend until the ice is pulverized and the drink is foamy.

Pour into tall glasses and serve icy cold, immediately.

Sweet variation: Omit saffron and hot water. Add 1 teaspoon of rosewater to the remaining ingredients.

YIELD: 2 10-ounce servings.

* Ratna Kolhatkar, who gave us the recipe, says that lassi in India is a much creamier drink due to the creaminess of Indian yogurt. She suggests the addition of heavy cream to approximate this texture, the trademark of the Indian lassi.

*Rich—and bursting
with fresh coconut flavor.*

Coconut Milk

1 coconut
3 cups boiling water

Pierce the three soft spots in the coconut with an ice pick or other sharp tool. Invert the coconut over a 2-cup measure and shake and drain until all the liquid is removed.

Heat the oven to 350°. Place the coconut on an oven rack and heat until the shell cracks in a few places, about 15 minutes. Wrap the coconut in a towel and strike with a hammer or other blunt tool. Pull the coconut meat out of the shell and pare off the brown skin with a swivel-bladed vegetable parer.

Place the reserved coconut liquid and the chunks of coconut in a food processor. Process until the coconut is finely ground.

Combine the ground coconut and boiling water in a bowl. Stir to blend. Cover and let stand for 1 hour.

Line a strainer with a triple thickness of dampened cheesecloth. Scrape the coconut and water into the strainer. Drain. Squeeze the cheesecloth to extract as much of the water and coconut flavor as possible.

Pour into a quart jar and refrigerate. Use within 2 days.

YIELD: about 1 quart.

A delicate, creamy,
sweet Caribbean import.

Mango and Coconut Shake

1 cup coconut milk (see page 66) *
1 cup peeled, sliced mango
½ cup cracked ice
Ground cardamom

Combine the coconut milk, mango, and ice in a blender. Whirl until the ice is pulverized and the drink is foamy. Pour into a tall glass. Sprinkle the top with ground cardamom.

YIELD: 1 generous serving, about 2 cups.

* The coconut milk adds a wonderful flavor here, but if it is not available, whole or low-fat milk or plain yogurt or vanilla yogurt can be substituted. Also, ripe cantaloupe, pineapple, or peaches can be substituted for the mango.

A rich, spicy Scandinavian warmer.

Hot Spiced
White Grape Glog

**2 bottles (750 ml./25.4 ounces each)
varietal white grape juice such as
Chenin Blanc or French Colombard
Zest of 1 orange, cut into a long spiral
1 slice fresh ginger, ¼ inch thick
⅓ cup golden raisins
5 whole cardamom seeds
¼ cup blanched, slivered almonds**

Combine the grape juice, orange zest, ginger,
raisins, and cardamom in a large saucepan. Heat
to boiling; cover and simmer for 1 hour. Just before
serving, add the almonds. Ladle into mugs and
serve with small spoons to scoop up the raisins
and almonds in the bottom of the cup.

YIELD: 8 6-ounce servings.

SERVE WITH: An array of your favorite cookies.

THE MOCKTAIL PARTY

Drink-and-clink parties aren't what they used to be —in fact, now they're even better! Savvy hosts have put the happiness back into the happy hour by keeping plenty of energizing, sophisticated alcohol-free potables on tap. The result? High spirits that *stay* high from the first refreshing sip to the last nip of the night; good mixers—lively, festive guests who will last as long as the party roars on, and the kind of kick that just can't come from a bottle.

Serve these nippy "straight" renditions of classic cocktails with a feast of hors d'oeuvres from your favorite takeout gourmet shop—savory country pâté, wedges of Cheddar cheese from mild to sharp, brioche mounded with spicy curried chicken —and your happy hour may continue all night long.

A coconutty delight.

Coco Colada

**8-ounce can pineapple chunks or crushed
   pineapple in unsweetened juice, frozen
   solid ***
1 cup cold water
½ cup canned cream of coconut **
**1 bottle (750 ml./25.4 ounces) seltzer
   water, well chilled**
Mint leaves

Transfer the solid mass from the can of pineapple to a blender or food processor. Add water
and cream of coconut. Whirl in the blender about
1 minute, or until the mixture is creamy. Half-fill a
6-cup pitcher with the mixture. Top with seltzer
water. Serve in oversize martini glasses garnished
with mint leaves.

YIELD: by the pitcher (1½ quarts).

SERVE WITH: Tortilla chips and bowls of salsa verde,
chunky guacamole, and salsa roja for dipping.

* Keep an 8-ounce can of pineapple ready in the freezer. (It
will make 5 8-ounce drinks.) By the way, frozen pineapple,
whirled in the blender solo, produces a very refreshing ice.
** Canned cream of coconut is available in 15-ounce cans.
Shake well before opening. If the can has been stored in a
cool spot, the coconut fat may be solid. If so, heat the can
gently in a saucepan of warm water; then shake the can well
to blend. (See page 49 for storing leftover cream of coconut.)

*A very adult adaptation
of a cocktail hour classic.*

Earl Grey Sour

⅔ cup strong, freshly brewed Earl Grey
   tea, chilled *
3 tablespoons *each* freshly squeezed
   lemon and orange juice
2 tablespoons sugar
½ cup cracked ice
1 egg white
Orange zest spirals

Combine the tea, lemon juice, orange juice, sugar, cracked ice, and egg white in a blender. Whirl for 1 full minute to completely pulverize the ice. Pour into 2 rocks glasses and garnish each with an orange peel spiral.

YIELD: 2 8-ounce drinks.

SERVE WITH: Cold sesame noodles or fried Chinese dumplings.

* See Making Iced Tea, page 91.

*As nippy and refreshing
as the ocean-side surf.*

Cape Cod Revisited

**3 ounces cranberry juice (for real cranberry
    juice, see page 136)**
**3 ounces still white grape juice such as
    Chenin Blanc, French Colombard, or a
    blend, well chilled ***
Orange zest spiral
Ice

Over ice in rocks glass, add equal parts cranberry and grape juices. Twist the orange spiral to release the flavorful oils. Drape over ice and the side of the glass.

YIELD: 1 8-ounce serving.

SERVE WITH: Barbecued chicken wings and celery sticks with tangy bleu cheese dip.

* Varietal grape juice is available in 750 ml./25.4-fluid-ounce bottles. Cranberry juice is available in 1-quart bottles. One bottle of each is enough for 8 8-ounce servings.

Varietal Grape Juice Spritzer

Ice cubes
6 ounces still white grape juice such as
    Chenin Blanc, French Colombard, or a
    blend, well chilled *
Seltzer or other sparkling waters, plain or
    flavored with orange, lemon, or lime
Lemon, lime, or orange slices.

Select a wine glass or a tall glass. Add ice cubes and grape juice. Top off with seltzer or sparkling water. Garnish as desired with lemon, lime, or orange slices.

YIELD: 1 8-ounce serving.

SERVE WITH: Dry-roasted mixed nuts or slices of country pâté served with crackers and tiny sour gherkins. These spritzers mix beautifully with nearly any food.

* Varietal grape juice is available in 750 ml./25.4-fluid-ounce bottles. One bottle of grape juice will make 4 spritzers. One liter of seltzer or sparkling water is more than sufficient for 4 servings.

The perfect cooler for Derby Day
or any warm late afternoon.

Lime and Mint Julep

3 tablespoons mint syrup (see page 75)
1 cup crushed ice
3 tablespoons freshly squeezed lime juice
Fresh mint sprigs

Heap ice into a rocks glass. Pour mint syrup and lime juice over the ice.

Garnish with a sprig of mint and serve with a thin, short bar straw to stir and sip. For an interesting variation, substitute ginger syrup (page 113) for mint.

YIELD: 1 8-ounce serving.

SERVE WITH: Pita bread stuffed with spinach, mushroom, and alfalfa sprout salad.

Mint Syrup

1 cup sugar
1 cup water
¼ cup coarsely chopped fresh mint leaves
    and stems, packed into a cup

Combine the sugar and water in a small saucepan.

Heat, stirring, over medium heat until the sugar dissolves. Stir in the mint. Cover and simmer over very low heat for 10 minutes.

Let stand, covered, at room temperature, overnight.

Transfer to a pint jar and refrigerate until ready to serve. Recipe can be doubled or tripled.

YIELD: 1⅓ cups, or enough syrup for 6 Lime and Mint Juleps.

ENERGY-POWERED
After-Workout Boosters

You're working hard to pump up, slim down, to peak out on a healthy high. But how to deliciously nourish and replenish the body you've pushed to the limit?

Lift these natural revitalizers after each conditioning session and your body will get the fuel it needs to go the distance—and beyond! These flavor-packed boosters restore energy levels, revive flagging stamina, and give you vitamins to burn.

Now exercise that elbow for a real power lift!

A cooling sparkling refresher
with a snappy twist.

Pear and Ginger Beer

12-ounce can pear nectar, well chilled
12-ounce bottle ginger beer, well chilled
Juice of 1 lime
Ice cubes
Lime slices

Pour the pear nectar, ginger beer, and lime juice into a pitcher half-filled with ice. Stir to blend. Pour into tall glasses and garnish with lime slices.

YIELD: 1 quart.

SERVE WITH: Ripe, juicy pears, cored, cut into wedges, and sprinkled with lime juice.

Tart and tangy, this creamy cooler
gets your second wind gusting.

Pink Buttermilk with Basil

2 tomato juice ice cubes (see below)
12 ounces buttermilk
2 small basil leaves
2 sprigs basil

Combine the ice cubes, buttermilk, and basil leaves in a blender. Whirl until the ice is smooth. Pour into tall glasses and garnish each with a sprig of basil.

YIELD: 2 8-ounce servings.

SERVE WITH: Bowl of iced celery sticks, green pepper wedges, and cherry tomatoes for a one/two energy punch.

Tomato Juice Ice Cubes

Pour 2 cups of tomato juice into an ice cube tray. Freeze. When solid, transfer the cubes to a plastic bag and keep ready in the freezer.

An after-exercise reviver that takes you from down-and-out to up-and-at 'em in a few invigorating gulps.

Chocolate Banana Shake

1 cup low-fat milk
1 cup low-fat plain yogurt
1 small, ripe banana (about ½ cup, cut up)
2 tablespoons chocolate syrup
¼ teaspoon vanilla extract

Combine all the ingredients in a blender; puree until smooth. Pour into a tall glass and enjoy.

YIELD: 1 generous serving, about 2 cups.

Fresh Tomato Froth

8 ounces ripe, juicy tomatoes (1 large or 2
   small), cut up and cored
2 ice cubes, cracked into smallish pieces
¼ medium green bell pepper, seeds
   removed, cut into chunks
½ small cucumber, pared, seeds removed,
   cut into chunks
¼ teaspoon salt
¼ teaspoon cumin, or to taste
1 sprig cilantro (fresh coriander), cut up
Dash of hot pepper sauce
2 scallions, washed, trimmed, and left
   whole

Puree the tomatoes, ice cubes, bell pepper,
cucumber, salt, cumin, cilantro, and hot pepper
sauce in a blender. Pour into 2 tall glasses and
serve with scallion swizzlers.

YIELD: 2 8-ounce servings.

SERVE WITH: Dish of nutmeg-laced large-curd cottage cheese for a satisfying lunch. And do nibble
the white part of the scallion as you sip the drink.

*While working for the "burn," dream of this
creamy, invigorating reward.*

Two-Berry Yogurt Cooler

1 cup rinsed, hulled, halved strawberries
1 cup real cranberry juice (see page 136)
½ cup plain yogurt
½ cup cracked ice

Combine all the ingredients in a blender.
Whirl until pureed. Pour into a tall glass and serve
with a straw.

YIELD: 1 generous serving, 2 cups.

SERVE WITH: Bowl of luscious ripe strawberries.
(Want to dip those berries in a bit of superfine
granulated sugar? Promise yourself you'll work it
off tomorrow.)

Strawberry-Banana Milk

1 cup rinsed, stemmed, sliced
   strawberries *
1 ripe banana
1 tablespoon sugar (optional)
1 cup low-fat milk
½ teaspoon vanilla extract
½ cup cracked ice

Combine all the ingredients in a blender;
puree. Pour into a tall glass.

YIELD: 2 10-ounce servings.

* When these fruits are out of season, use 1 cup of frozen
unsweetened sliced strawberries.

Everything about tofu is good—bean curd is high in protein, low in fat, and bland, the one characteristic that makes for culinary magic. In this energy-powered cooler, adaptable tofu takes on the flavor of the sweet, tart pineapple it is teamed with to produce a revitalizer that is every bit as good-tasting as it is good for you.

Tofu and Pineapple Cooler

1 cup fresh pineapple chunks
1 cup orange juice
4 ounces tofu, cut into ½-inch chunks
  (about ½ cup)
½ cup cracked ice
Orange slice

Combine pineapple chunks, orange juice, tofu, and ice in a blender. Whirl until the mixture is creamy, about 2 full minutes. Pour into a tall glass. Garnish with an orange slice.

YIELD: 1 12-ounce serving.

Dried Fruit-Sweetened Banana Health Shake

1 cup orange juice
½ cup buttermilk or low-fat yogurt
1 banana, peeled and cut up
4 dates, dried apricots, pitted prunes, or
    2 tablespoons raisins
1 tablespoon wheat germ

Combine all the ingredients in a blender; whirl until thoroughly blended, at least 1 minute. Pour into a tall glass and enjoy.

YIELD: about 2½ cups, or 2 10-ounce servings.

*A smooth, icy drink
that is refreshing and cooling.*

Fig Frappe

4 fresh, ripe Kadota figs, stems trimmed *
¼ cup orange juice
1 cup plain yogurt
½ cup crushed ice **
Orange slice

In a blender, combine figs, orange juice, yogurt, and ice. Blend until the mixture is very smooth. Pour into a tall glass and garnish with an orange slice.

YIELD: 1 generous serving, about 2 cups.

* Fresh figs are in season in late summer and early fall. Figs canned in light syrup can be substituted, but are not quite the same.
** For a slightly different twist, omit the crushed ice and substitute 8 ounces of plain frozen yogurt. The yield will be a little smaller.

A TAILGATE PARTY

Americans have been sideswiped by tailgate fever (and if you don't believe us, check with your own state police). People are packing up their parties and taking them on the road in record numbers, celebrating the journey as well as the destination. And why not—enroute to every vacation hideway there's a sunny turnabout just big enough to serve as a picnic spot. Even a winter trek to the lift lines in enlivened by a warming detour spent listening to the radio and cuddling up to a cup that thaws the hands and sparks enthusiasm.

But scenic overlooks and rest areas away from the madding 60-mph crowd cannot compare with the kind of rousing tailgate free-for-all that celebrates its own homeliness to the max—the parking lot party. Avid baseball and football fans have elevated between-the-white-lines galas to an art form, filling these "asphalt patios" with the aroma of peppery grilled meat, and a feeling of lusty camaraderie that flows from fender to bumper and straight through the gates.

Hearty is the byword for packing the tailgate meal: opt for stick-to-the-ribs sandwiches, chunky, sharp cheeses, old-time spice desserts, and you'll satisfy those ravenous appetites whetted by the great outdoors. Then wash down that good food— and those contagious good feelings—with these quenching tailgate tipplers and hit the road—safely.

Grape and Lime Cooler

24-ounce bottle purple grape juice
24-ounce bottle white grape juice
¼ cup fresh lime juice
1 lime, sliced thin
2 cups ice cubes*

Combine the purple and white grape juices
and lime juice in a thermos. Stir to blend. Add the
lime slices and enough ice to fill the thermos.

YIELD: 1½ quarts.

SERVE WITH: Seedless ruby and green grapes and
brown-edged sugar cookies.

* For a more intense flavor, freeze 2 cups of limeade (page
106) in an ice cube tray. When solid, place in plastic bag and
keep ready in the freezer.

*Accelerate your rubberneck tour
with this natural refresher.*

Real Orangeade

1 quart orange juice, preferably freshly
    squeezed (for the best flavor, try not to
    use juice made from concentrate)
Juice of 1 lemon
½ cup simple syrup, chilled (see below)
1 juice orange, coarsely chopped (½-inch
    pieces, seeds removed)
1 quart ice cubes

Pour the orange and lemon juices and syrup
into a 2-quart thermos. Stir to blend. Add the orange pieces and enough ice to fill the thermos.
Stir well with a wooden spoon so that the orange
skins are bruised, releasing the aromatic oils.

YIELD: 2 quarts.

Simple Syrup

Stir ½ cup of sugar and 1 cup of water together in
a small saucepan. Heat to boiling, stirring often, to
dissolve the sugar. Cover and simmer for 5 minutes. Let stand off the heat, covered, for 5 minutes
more.

Pour into a jar and refrigerate until very cold.
Syrup can be made up to 2 weeks ahead and kept
in the refrigerator at the ready.

YIELD: 1⅓ cups.

A flavorful weatherproofer for gridiron fans or skiers heading for that early morning schuss.

Hot Apple-Spiced Tea

2 quarts unfiltered apple juice
4 orange-spice herbal tea bags
1 cinnamon stick
2 strips (½ x 2 inches) orange zest

Combine the apple juice, tea bags, and cinnamon stick in a saucepan. Heat slowly over medium-low heat until simmering. Do not boil. Steep for 5 minutes. Remove the tea bags.

Add the orange zest. Cover; simmer for 5 minutes. Pour into a thermos.

YIELD: 2 quarts.

SERVE WITH: Wedges of applesauce spice cake or lemon-flavored poppy seed cake.

For a refreshing blast that will hit the spot, pack this tangy cooler when you hit the road.

Iced Lemon Tea

1 quart tea (see Making Iced Tea, page 91)
6-ounce can frozen lemonade,
   reconstituted according to package
   directions
1 lemon, cut into wedges, seeds removed
2 cups ice cubes

Combine the tea and lemonade in a thermos. If more convenient, reconstitute the lemonade right in the insulated bottle, then add the tea.

Squeeze the lemon wedges into the thermos; add the pieces of lemon after squeezing.

Add enough ice to fill the thermos.

YIELD: 2 quarts.

SERVE WITH: Soft dinner rolls filled with curried chicken salad or a tuna and Muenster cheese salad on leaves of Boston lettuce.

Making Iced Tea

Method 1: Place 3 tea bags in a quart jar; fill with cool tap water. Let stand in a sunny window or outdoors until brewed (at least 1 hour).

Method 2: Place 3 tea bags in a quart jar. Add very hot tap water. Let stand until brewed (at least 30 minutes). Cool at room temperature.

Method 3: Place 3 tea bags in a teapot. Add 1 quart of boiling water. Let steep for 10 minutes. Remove tea bags and cool at room temperature until ready to use.

Tip: To clear refrigerated tea that has turned cloudy, boil some water and gradually pour it into the clouded tea until the tea shows signs of clearing. About ½ cup should do the trick for 1 quart of tea. YIELD: 1 quart.

How to Brew a Pot of Tea

Start with cold water. Do not use water that has been sitting around at room temperature or that has previously been boiled.

Place the tea of your choice, preferably loose, in a teapot that has been rinsed with hot water (tea that steeps in a cold pot will cool off). Pour the boiling water over the tea; cover and let steep for 3 to 4 minutes. Cover the pot with a kitchen towel or a tea cozy to keep it warm.

Stir the tea briskly, then pour into cups through a tea strainer to catch the floating leaves. Serve with a separate pitcher of hot milk or half and half and sugar. You might like to serve a small pot of hot water so that sippers can dilute the tea to their taste.

*This hot chocolate drink is really meant for
the younger set, though a few of us
thoroughly mellowed others might be
tempted as well. Not for the purist—whether
young or young-at-heart—but chock full of
lip-smacking goodness for the
cold and thirsty.*

Hot Chocolate Milk

**2 quarts commercially prepared chocolate
milk**
or
**2 quarts milk plus 1 cup (or to taste)
chocolate-flavored syrup**
1 cinnamon stick
2 teaspoons vanilla extract

Pour prepared chocolate milk into a large
saucepan. (If using milk and syrup, combine them
in a saucepan.) Add the cinnamon stick.

Heat, stirring to prevent sticking, over medium-
low heat until simmering. Remove from heat.

Remove the cinnamon stick. Stir in the vanilla
extract. Pour into a thermos.

YIELD: 2 quarts.

SERVE WITH: Gooey brownies.

A JUNE WEDDING

What is even warmer than an early summer's day? A wedding. No other occasion, no matter how festive, can rival the happy nuptial celebration.

If you are lucky enough to be hosting this summer's most beautiful rite of passage, take heart—any small culinary misadventures lose their impact in the presence of a radiant bride. But long before you even begin to plan the menu, look outside: the trees have grown lush and green, the roses are climbing the trellis. Can you think of a better setting in which to toast the happy couple?

But if space does not permit (or if a summer shower chases your festivities inside), be sure to bring a bit of that natural splendor indoors along with you. Happy feelings bloom when flowers abound—so vase them, arrange them, nestle them among the hors d'oeuvres, and use them to crown that spectacular cake.

Don't overlook the little touches that give your celebration an elegant lift. Bring out your best—gleaming crystal, delicate bone china, your heirloom silver—and add that final touch of polish to a day that was meant to shine.

Then unveil the sophisticated punches and spritzers that guests will raise again and again to both the happy couple and an event to remember.

*An elegant little drink
that bursts with beautiful color.*

Fresh Raspberry Spritz

**2 half-pints fresh raspberries
2 tablespoons sugar
1 tablespoon fresh lemon juice
Seltzer water, well chilled *
White grape juice, well chilled *
Fresh raspberries or mint sprigs (optional)**

Puree the raspberries, sugar, and lemon juice in a food processor or blender. (It should make about 2 cups.) Push through a fine sieve to remove the seeds. The puree can be stored, tightly covered, in the refrigerator for 1 or 2 days or frozen for up to 3 months.

To serve, place 1 tablespoon of the raspberry puree in the bottom of a champagne glass. Fill with half seltzer water and half white-grape juice. Garnish the glass with 4 raspberries on a small plastic straw, or mint leaves if desired.

Make sure the seltzer and grape juice are well chilled. In fact, keep them on hand in ice buckets or a large silver or crystal bowl filled with ice.

YIELD: 16 6-ounce drinks.

SERVE WITH: Sausage en croûte, cold salmon with cucumber-dill sauce, and avocado, grapefruit, and spinach salad.

* For 16 6-ounce servings you will need about 1½ quarts each of seltzer water and white grape juice.

94

*A fresh, natural punch ideal
for toasting the bride and groom.*

Bubbling Strawberry Punch

10-ounce package frozen strawberries in
  light syrup
2 cups orange juice
1 tray orange ice cubes (see below)
1 bottle (1 liter/33.8 fluid ounces) orange-
  flavored sparkling water or seltzer water
6 orange slices

Thaw the strawberries according to package
directions. Puree strawberries in a food processor
or blender. In large glass pitcher (about 2 quarts),
combine strawberries, orange juice, and orange
ice cubes. Slowly add the sparkling water or
seltzer. Garnish each all-purpose wine glass with
an orange slice.

YIELD: 6 10-ounce servings.

SERVE WITH: An enormous platter of raw vegetables. Start with a base of endive, radicchio, and
bibb lettuce. Add strips of red and green bell pepper, fennel, zucchini, cherry tomatoes, radishes,
carrots, and blanched asparagus spears and green
beans. Accompany with Bagna Cauda, a rich olive
oil and anchovy dip.

Orange Ice Cubes

Combine juice and zest of 1 orange with 1½ cups
of water. Pour into an ice cube tray and freeze.
When solid, place in a plastic bag and keep on
hand in the freezer.

Sparkling Grape Punch

Frozen grape ring (see page 14)
1 bottle (750 ml/25.4 fluid ounces) white
    varietal grape juice such as Chenin
    Blanc or French Colombard
1 bottle (750 ml/25.4 fluid ounces)
    sparkling white grape juice such as
    Catawba, well chilled
1 bottle (1 liter/33.8 fluid ounces) seltzer
    water, well chilled

Prepare grape ring a day ahead; add a few
whole strawberries for a color accent, if desired.

Just before serving, combine the juices and
seltzer water in a large chilled (if possible) punch
bowl. Carefully unmold the ring of ice and fruit and
float it in the punch. Serve in all-purpose wine
glasses or punch cups.

YIELD: about 14 6-ounce servings.

SERVE WITH: Cold, rare filet of beef with rémoulade
sauce and a watercress, mushroom, and walnut
salad.

A GOOD BOOK
AND A
TALL GLASS

Remember how summer used to be? Long days spent watching the clouds drift past or lazily eyeing the micro-industry of an anthill, imprinting your elbows and knees with the texture of the newly mown grass. However long ago those all-too-short sultry summer days seem now, they have stayed somehow fresh in the memory.

Balmy weather doesn't come with those options anymore, it seems. Your own home is an anthill of frenetic activity. And worse yet, the newly mown grass gives you hives (as does the mowing itself).

Still, there is one peaceful retreat, one oasis of glorious isolation still available to those of us who have climbed the hills of childhood and are now backing down the other side: a good book. Take that riveting thriller or hefty saga straight to the first quiet spot you find and dive right in—and when you come up for refreshment, reach for these airy summer coolers. They're every bit as lush as your memories of summers past.

A long, tall cooler that is nutritious as well as thirst-quenching. The repeating orange flavor —from the juice and zest—is just the thing to have while rereading that favorite classic.

Tomato and Orange Cooler with Basil

1 cup tomato juice *
½ cup orange juice, preferably freshly squeezed
Ice cubes
1 piece (½ by 1½ inches) orange zest
1 sprig fresh basil

Combine the tomato and orange juices in a tall glass (for one) or 2 rocks glasses (for two quiet readers); add 2 ice cubes. Twist the piece of orange zest to release the flavorful oils, then add to the glass. Garnish with a sprig of fresh basil.

YIELD: 1 12-ounce serving (2 6-ounce servings).

SERVE WITH: Carrot sticks slathered with a tangy yogurt-based herb dip.

* For fresh tomato juice see recipe page 99.

*Tomato lovers can't get their fill of this
remarkably easy-to-prepare refresher.*

Fresh Tomato Juice

**2 pounds ripe, juicy tomatoes, washed and
  quartered
1 thick slice onion
1 leafy celery top
1 full sprig of basil
2 cups water
Pinch of salt, or to taste**

Combine the tomatoes, onion, celery top,
basil, and water in a saucepan. Heat to boiling.

Cover and simmer over low heat for 30 minutes.
Puree the tomato mixture through a food mill, dis-
carding skins and seeds. Add salt. Enjoy while hot,
or cool to room temperature and then refrigerate.
Delicious with a grinding of coarse-grained black
pepper directly onto each serving.

NOTE: Fresh tomato juice is very perishable. Prepare only what you can consume within two days.
(Recipe can be halved if a smaller batch is more
practical.)

YIELD: 1 quart.

Mike's, on DeKalb Avenue, in Brooklyn, New York serves up what we believe is the best lemonade to ever slide across a counter.

Mike's Lemonade

1 lemon
1 to 2 tablespoons sugar (to taste)
Almost boiling water
Ice

At Mike's they make the lemonade as follows. Into one tall metal milkshake container, squeeze by hand the juice of 1 lemon. Then add the sugar and a squirt of boiling water. Stir—the boiling water dissolves the sugar very quickly. Then add the lemon rinds to the metal container, about 1 to 1¼ cups of water (straight from the tap), and whirl in the milkshake machine. Pour the entire contents into a tall glass half filled with ice cubes.

If you don't have a milkshake machine, try this method. Into a canning jar with a tight-fitting lid (flat lid and screw band), squeeze the juice of 1 lemon. Add the sugar and some hot water from the tea kettle; stir to dissolve the sugar. Add the lemon rinds and 1 to 1¼ cups of tap water. Then stir as hard as you can with a wooden spoon, concentrating on bruising the zest of the lemon to release those flavorful oils. Screw on the top and shake the whole thing for about 45 seconds. Then pour everything, rinds included, into a tall glass half filled with ice.

YIELD: 1 10-ounce serving.

SERVE WITH: The softest, gooiest chocolate-chip cookies studded with walnuts.

You had that who-dunnit figured out by page 97, or the latest romantic sizzler failed to sweep you off your feet. Console yourself with this sparkling drink.

Blueberry Lemon Fizz

8 ounces blueberry nectar
1 lemon wedge
4 ounces lemon-flavored sparkling water
Ice cubes

Pour the blueberry nectar over ice in a very tall glass. Squeeze the lemon wedge into a glass; add the lemon pieces as well. Fill the glass with lemon-flavored sparkling water and stir.

YIELD: 1 12-ounce serving.

SERVE WITH: Lemon-flavored yogurt garnished with a spoonful of fresh blueberries.

When that thriller explodes into action, cool off with this pleasantly bitter thirst-quencher.

Tangerine and Tonic with Lime

6 ounces tangerine juice *
Ice cubes
1 lime wedge
2 to 3 ounces tonic or quinine water,
well chilled

Pour tangerine juice into a tall glass and add a few ice cubes. Squeeze the lime wedge into the glass and drop it in. Top with tonic water and serve with a straw.

YIELD: 1 10-ounce serving.

SERVE WITH: An assortment of green olives.

* Frozen tangerine juice concentrate is available in 6-ounce cans. One reconstituted can makes 4 10-ounce drinks.

Honey-Spiked Ginger Tea

4 cups cold water
1 slice fresh ginger, ¼ inch thick, cut from
   the widest part of the root
3 heaping teaspoons tea leaves, preferably
   Orange Pekoe or Darjeeling
Juice of 1 lemon
2 to 3 tablespoons honey, or to taste
Ice cubes
Mint sprigs

In a saucepan, slowly heat the water and ginger to boiling. Remove from the heat. Stir in the tea leaves. Cover and let steep, off the heat, for 3 to 4 minutes. Add the lemon juice and honey; stir to blend. Let stand at room temperature until cool. Pour over ice in tall glasses. Garnish each glass with a sprig of mint.

YIELD: 1 quart.

SERVE WITH: A platter of bar cookies such as hermits.

*Long and tall enough to keep you
happy from cover to cover.*

Peach and Lime Cooler

1 large, ripe, juicy peach, peeled and
  sliced
2 teaspoons sugar, or to taste
2 tablespoons lime juice
1 cup crushed ice
½ cup cold water
Lime slice
Fresh mint sprig

Combine the peach slices, sugar, lime juice, crushed ice, and cold water in a blender. Blend until the ingredients are liquefied, about 2 minutes. Pour into a tall glass, garnish with a lime slice and mint sprig, and serve with a straw.

YIELD: 1 16-ounce serving.

SERVE WITH: Thin-sliced fresh tomatoes on toast spread lightly with homemade mayonnaise. Garnish with fresh basil leaves.

JULY 4TH SPARKLERS
Summer Drinks for a Crowd

The weatherman has promised an All-American sultry summer day. The city has vowed to light up the sky just as soon as dusk—and those firecracking kids—settle. But the happy crowd you've gathered in your backyard is *your* responsibility, from the neighbor whose idea of starting the grill means tossing in a few cherry bombs to that riotous group of softball maniacs now rounding third right through your prized crop of zinnias. It's up to you to cool them off without dampening those high spirits.

Prime the pump with an array of fruits and julienned vegetables they can munch while waiting for the coals to burn down—then bring on America's favorite outdoor feast: hot dogs and hamburgers grilled to perfection, Grandma's tangy German potato salad, an earthenware pot of hearty baked beans, and lots and *lots* of corn on the cob, dripping with herb butter. Declare your independence from complicated dessert-making by pulling that old wooden ice cream freezer out of the basement and filling it with a rich, custardy base brimming with fresh summer fruits. Then let those rowdy revelers crank away, pausing to wet their whistles with some of these splashy temperature tamers, while you relax and watch the fun.

*Like starburst fireworks, the dusky smell of
charcoal, and the requisite brigade of ants,
this is a Fourth of July tradition.*

Limeade

**3 tablespoons limeade syrup (see page
   107)**
Lime ice (optional, see Note, page 107)
8 ounces cold water or seltzer water
Lime slices

Pour limeade syrup over ice into a tall glass.
Slowly fill the glass with cold water or seltzer, stirring to blend. Garnish with a lime slice.

For a 2½-quart pitcher (6 servings), use 1 cup
plus 2 tablespoons of syrup, 1 tray of ice cubes,
and 6 to 7 cups of water or seltzer.

YIELD: 1 10-ounce serving (or by the pitcher).

SERVE WITH: Traditional barbecue fare, or for a special treat, oatmeal-raisin cookies.

Limeade Syrup

1 cup sugar
1 cup water
1 cup fresh lime juice

Combine the sugar and water in a small saucepan. Heat to boiling, stir to dissolve the sugar. Cover and simmer for 5 minutes. Cool at room temperature. Add the lime juice. Refrigerate, tightly covered, until ready to use. (This syrup can be made with lemon juice as well.)

NOTE: This syrup can also be used to create fruit-flavored ice cubes. Use ¼ cup of syrup to 1¾ cups of water.

YIELD: 2⅓ cups syrup, enough for 7 10-ounce servings of limeade.

This drink was inspired by the celebrated Bellini, a fresh peach puree and sparkling white wine combination served at the famous Harry's bar in Venice.

Redesigned Bellini
by the Pitcher

**2 cups peeled, sliced, ripe and juicy
  peaches (reserve 1 peach pit)
¼ cup sugar
2 tablespoons lime juice
1 bottle (1 liter/33.8 ounces) seltzer water,
  well chilled
1 bottle (750 ml/25.4 fluid ounces)
  sparkling white grape juice, well chilled
Fresh raspberries (optional)**

In a bowl, toss the peaches with sugar and lime juice. Mash the peaches with the back of a spoon or transfer to a food processor or blender and puree. Place peaches in a tall pitcher. Add the reserved pit for flavor.

Slowly add the seltzer water and the sparkling white grape juice. Stir with a long-handled spoon. Pour into stemmed glasses, using the spoon to distribute the pulp evenly. Garnish each wine glass with a few raspberries, if desired.

YIELD: about 2 quarts, or 10 8-ounce servings.

SERVE WITH: Thin slices of cheesecake topped with sliced strawberries.

*Reminiscent of your favorite
tart/sweet seasonal pie.*

Clove-Scented Rhubarb Punch with Strawberries

**1 pound rhubarb stalks, washed, ends
    trimmed, cut into 1-inch lengths
4 whole cloves
2 cups water
¼ cup sugar, or to taste
Ice cubes
1 cup sliced strawberries
Ginger ale, well chilled (optional)**

Combine the rhubarb, 2 of the cloves, and water in a saucepan. Heat to boiling. Cover and simmer until the rhubarb is very soft, about 25 minutes.

Strain the rhubarb through a fine sieve; press on the pulp with the back of a spoon to extract as much juice and flavor as possible.

Add the sugar to the hot juice, stirring to dissolve. Add the remaining 2 cloves. Cool at room temperature. Refrigerate until ready to serve.

Half-fill a large pitcher with ice cubes; add strawberries. Add rhubarb juice and stir well. Top pitcher with ginger ale to taste, if desired.

YIELD: about 4 10-ounce servings, or 1 quart.

SERVE WITH: Crudités of fresh fruit: cantaloupe wedges, whole strawberries, and papaya wedges dipped in sweetened ricotta cheese spiked with cinnamon.

*As cool and refreshing as a dip
in that out-of-the-way stream.*

Spearmint Iced Tea

**2 tea bags, Orange Pekoe or another
  flavorful tea
1 spearmint tea bag
1 quart boiling water
2 tablespoons sugar, or to taste
Ice cubes
Mint or spearmint sprigs
Lemon wedges**

Combine boiling water and tea bags in heat-resistant jar, pitcher, or teapot (see Making Iced Tea, page 91). Stir in the sugar until dissolved, if using. Cool to room temperature.

To serve, pour over ice cubes in tall glasses. Garnish with a sprig of mint—spearmint, if available—and add a squirt of lemon juice.

YIELD: about 4 10-ounce servings, or 1 quart.

SERVE WITH: A dish of lemon sorbet or ice.

*For a long, refreshing blast of that
most wonderful of all the summer fruits.*

Raspberry Iced Tea

**1 quart boiling water
2 Orange Pekoe tea bags
⅓ cup raspberry syrup *
Fresh mint sprigs**

Combine the boiling water and tea bags in a heat-resistant jar, pitcher, or teapot (see Making Iced Tea, page 91). Stir in the syrup and a sprig of mint; bruise the mint with the back of a spoon to release its flavor.

Cool at room temperature. To serve, pour over ice and garnish each tall glass with a sprig of mint.

YIELD: about 4 10-ounce servings, or 1 quart.

SERVE WITH: A bowl of fresh red raspberries served au naturel or with raspberry jam-filled cookies, a miniature version of the wonderful Linzer Tarte.

* Imported from Europe and available in specialty food shops.

Real Ginger Ale

**2 tablespoons ginger syrup (see
   page 113)
Ice cubes
Seltzer water, well chilled**

Half-fill a tall glass with ice cubes. Add ginger syrup. Slowly add the cold seltzer water. Stir gently to mix.

Garnish with a slice of kiwi or carambola (star fruit).

YIELD: 1 10-ounce serving.

SERVE WITH: A big bowl of pistachio nuts.

Ginger Syrup

4 ounces fresh ginger, pared and
   cut into ½-inch chunks
2½ cups water
1¼ cups sugar

Finely chop the ginger and 1 cup of water in a food processor or blender. Transfer to a medium saucepan.

Add the remaining water and heat to boiling; cover and simmer over low heat for 10 minutes. Take off the heat and let stand, covered, overnight, or for at least 12 hours.

Strain through a fine sieve or a sieve lined with a double thickness of dampened cheesecloth. Squeeze the cheesecloth to extract all the liquid from the ginger. Discard the cheesecloth and ginger.

Return the liquid to the saucepan. Stir in the sugar; heat slowly to a boil, stirring to dissolve the sugar; cover and simmer over low heat for 10 minutes. Uncover, heat to boiling. Boil until reduced to about 2 cups, about 10 minutes. Pour into a pint jar, seal, and cool at room temperature.

Store in the refrigerator for up to 1 month to use as a flavoring for drinks or as a dessert sauce.

YIELD: about 2 cups.

Peach, Orange, and Ginger Fizz

**10-ounce package frozen peaches
  in light syrup
2 cups orange juice
Ice cubes (optional)
Ginger ale, well chilled
Orange slices**

Thaw the peaches according to package directions. Puree in a food processor or blender. Divide the peach puree evenly among 4 tall glasses. Add ½ cup of orange juice to each glass, and ice cubes, if desired. Top off with a slow stream of ginger ale. Stir gently to mix. Garnish with orange slices.

YIELD: 4 10-ounce servings.

SERVE WITH: Peach ice cream.

For Marie Simmons, Nana's tea was a childhood staple. Nana, who is now 93 years young, dictated this recipe so that we could include it in this collection.

Nana's Tea

2 quarts plus 1 pint cold water
½ cup Orange Pekoe tea leaves *
Handful of fresh mint leaves plus extra
   for garnish
⅓ cup sugar, or to taste
Water
½ cup bottled lemon juice
1 orange, quartered
Ice cubes

In a saucepan, combine the water, tea leaves, and mint leaves. Slowly heat to a boil; steep, covered, for 15 minutes. Strain through a sieve. (Save the tea leaves to use as mulch in the garden.) Cool the tea "stock" at room temperature. Refrigerate in jars until ready to serve.**

To serve, place the sugar and an equal amount of hot tap water in a large pitcher. Stir with a spoon to dissolve. Add 2 cups of cold water, 1 cup of tea stock, lemon juice, and orange quarters, gently squeezed. Stir with a large spoon. Add half a tray of ice cubes and mint leaves. Pour into tall glasses.

YIELD: 10 cups tea stock (or 10 1-quart pitchers).

SERVE WITH: Prune-filled sugar cookies, as Nana does. Also good with pecan sandies.

* Or 18 tea bags, if loose tea is not available.
** Stock keeps in the refrigerator for up to 1 week. It will become cloudy, but this will not affect the flavor.

Lemonade by the Pitcher

4 lemons
½ cup sugar
1½ quarts water
1 tray ice cubes
Pinch of grated nutmeg
Fresh mint sprig

Slice 1 lemon into ⅛-inch slices. Place in a large pitcher; add the sugar. Press and stir the lemon slices and sugar together until the sugar is dampened with lemon juice and the lemon rinds are well bruised. Let stand for about 15 minutes.

Squeeze the juice from 3 lemons. Add the lemon juice, water, ice, nutmeg, and mint sprig to the pitcher. Stir well to blend.

YIELD: about 8 10-ounce servings, or 2 quarts.

SERVE WITH: A plate of gingersnaps.

ON THE PORCH

Travel through any of New England's quiet by-ways, meander along the sleepy, scenic avenues that network the Midwest, drive down the kind of homey, welcoming streets named for the trees that shade them, and you'll see two hundred years of traditional homespun wisdom. The front porch, whether a plain clapboard promontory or an elegant perch embellished with curls of Victorian gingerbread, was Great-Grandad's affirmation that pioneering Americans were meant to live indoors *and out*.

Settle into that ladder-backed rocker to catch the stray summer breeze—and a restful glimpse of the world slowly strolling by.

The porch was made for enthusiastic on-looking, whether you're silently umpiring a sidewalk stickball game or watching a late afternoon thunderstorm light up the cloudy sky. When the show falters, don't hesitate to nod off like Grandpa did. But when the action resumes, have some of these snappy refreshers close at hand. Like a lazy day on the porch, they'll make you feel good inside and out.

A flavorful pick-me-up that sharpens the eyes of front-porch supervisors everywhere.

Currant Juice

2 cups fresh currants, rinsed and
  stemmed *
⅓ cup superfine granulated sugar
3 cups water
Ice cubes
Lemon or lime wedges

Place the currants, sugar, and half of the water in a blender or food processor. Whirl until the currants are pureed. Add the remaining water and let stand at room temperature for about 1 hour.

Strain through a fine sieve, pressing on the pulp to extract as much of the flavor as possible, and transfer to a clean jar. This juice will keep for several days under refrigeration.

To serve, pour over ice in a tall glass and add a squirt of lemon or lime juice, if desired.

YIELD: about 4 10-ounce servings, or 1 quart.

SERVE WITH: A mélange of seasonal melons.

* Currants are available midsummer at farmers' markets.

Currant Cream

Here's a delicious, sweeter variation.

In a blender, whip together 1 cup of currant juice, ¼ cup heavy cream, and ¼ cup of cracked ice. Serve in a tall glass with a straw.

YIELD: 1 10-ounce serving.

*A summertime eye-opener that
is nearly a meal in itself.*

Coffee Yogurt Soda

½ cup (4 ounces) plain or coffee-flavored
   yogurt, or half and half
1 10-ounce bottle coffee soda
Coffee ice cubes (optional) *

Stir the yogurt in the bottom of a tall glass
until smooth. Gradually stir in the coffee soda so
that the mixture remains smooth and creamy. Add
ice cubes, if desired.

YIELD: 1 12-ounce serving.

* Use 2 cups of coffee to make 1 tray of ice.

Cooling, satisfying, and soothing, this porch cooler is more than enough all by itself.

Double Papaya Frappe

1 cup papaya juice
1 ripe papaya, seeds and skin removed,
   cut up
½ cup crushed ice
1 tablespoon lime juice
2 lime slices

Puree all the ingredients in a blender until frothy. Pour into a wine glass and garnish with a lime slice. Serve with a short straw (to make it last longer).

YIELD: 2 8-ounce servings.

SERVE WITH: Slices of fresh fruit such as apples and pears.

* Papaya juice is often sold as a blend of juices and could include apple, pear, or grape—any combination you happen to find will do.

A tall vegetable-based sparkler to nurse while less-fortunate neighbors mow their lawns.

Thyme-Scented Tomato Tonic Cooler

8 ounces tomato juice
2 tablespoons lime juice
Tomato juice ice cubes (see page 78) or
    plain ice cubes
4 ounces tonic water, well chilled
1 sprig fresh thyme
1 lime slice

Combine the tomato juice and the lime juice in a tall glass. Add a few ice cubes. Stir in the tonic water. Bruise thyme leaves with your fingers and add to the glass. Garnish with a slice of lime.

YIELD: 1 12-ounce serving.

SERVE WITH: Open-faced sliced cucumber and sweet butter sandwiches on whole-grain bread, garnished with sprigs of fresh dill.

*Mix up this heady brew and you won't care
that the weeds are growing faster
than the flowers.*

Vanilla-Scented Iced Tea with Lemon

1 quart boiling water
2 tea bags
2 tablespoons sugar, or to taste
1 teaspoon vanilla extract
Ice cubes
Fresh lemon balm leaves or twist of lemon
    zest

Combine the boiling water and tea bags in a heat-resistant jar, pitcher, or teapot (see How to Brew a Pot of Tea, page 91). Add the sugar; stir to dissolve. Cool to room temperature. Add the vanilla.

Fill tall glasses with ice. Add the tea. Garnish with lemon balm or a twist of lemon zest.

The vanilla gives the illusion of sweetness, so hold back a little on the sugar; taste, then add more if your palate demands it.

YIELD: about 4 10-ounce servings, or 1 quart.

SERVE WITH: A plate of lemon cookies, although it's very satisfying without any accompaniment at all.

It's August and that first cool blast of autumn is ruffling the awnings. Usher it in with this soda-lover's special.

Maple Spritzer

2 tablespoons pure maple syrup
3 or 4 lemon or orange ice cubes (see below)
8 to 10 ounces seltzer water, well chilled

Spoon the syrup into a tall glass. Add the ice cubes. Slowly add the seltzer water, stirring gently to blend.

YIELD: 1 10-ounce serving.

SERVE WITH: A dish of coffee ice cream.

Lemon or Orange Ice Cubes

Zest and juice of 1 lemon or orange
Cold water
1 tablespoon sugar (optional)

Combine the juice and the zest of 1 lemon or orange in a 2-cup measure. Add enough water to measure 2 cups total. Add sugar, if desired.

Pour into an ice cube tray. When solid, transfer to a plastic bag, seal with a twist-tie, and keep ready for later use.

SODA FOUNTAIN SPECIALS

Shame on those killjoys who would deprive kids of all ages the pleasures of a discerning sweet tooth! Health is meant to be enjoyed to the fullest and that means allowing yourself a languid afternoon spent sipping a rich delight, spooning that creamy foam out of the bottom of a tall glass, and reveling in that satisfying slurp as your straw seeks out the very last drop of a smooth, frothy shake.

The longer we live, the more we are convinced that these soda-fountain treats are the curative waters of our day, building better morale in more ways than one. Our classic Root Beer Float will set your cares adrift; our old-time corner-drugstore egg creams are guaranteed to soothe away whatever ails you. Share your well-deserved indulgence with friends and you'll double the bubbling good spirits.

For a classic fountain touch, keep plenty of flexible straws in an apothecary jar and serve your fizzes and rickeys in the tallest hurricane glasses you can find. Let guests dangle their feet from waist-high bar stools while they sip. And don't forget to buy your seltzer the old-fashioned way, in green or blue glass bottles, complete with the hit-or-miss classic spigot on the top.

Then sip away like you did at the corner store, nursing these tall, creamy soda fountain specials so they last . . . and last . . . and last!

The question is, when to add the chocolate syrup. We offer two versions of this soda fountain classic, both rich mixtures of chocolate syrup, milk, and seltzer, well chilled. The difference is in the order in which the ingredients are combined. (Just for the record, we prefer version A, but version B is offered for those who may beg to differ.)

Chocolate Egg Cream

2 tablespoons chocolate-flavored syrup *
¼ cup cold milk
Seltzer water, well chilled

Version A

Stir the chocolate syrup and milk together until well blended. Squirt in the seltzer water if you are lucky enough to have a real seltzer bottle, or pour it in, stirring vigorously with a long-handled spoon to blend. (Don't stop stirring until a nice foamy head has formed on the top of the glass.)

Version B

Combine the milk and the seltzer in a tall glass, then stir in the chocolate syrup until the drink is blended and a head forms.

YIELD: 1 10-ounce serving.

* Fox's U-Bet is the classic choice but any thin chocolate-flavored syrup will do.

*A sparkling, bubbly refresher
with a bold, citrusy bite.*

Lime Rickey

Ice cubes
½ lime
Cherry syrup
Seltzer water, well chilled.

Fill a tall glass with ice cubes. Squeeze the juice from the lime half directly into the glass and add the lime half as well. Add a shot of cherry syrup, about 2 tablespoons, then fill the glass with seltzer. Stir well with a long-handled spoon.

YIELD: 1 10-ounce serving.

Root Beer Float

Vanilla ice cream
Root beer, chilled

Drop a hefty scoop of vanilla ice cream into a tall glass. Slowly add enough root beer to half-fill the glass. Stir the ice cream and soda together to soften the ice cream slightly. Slowly fill the glass with root beer, forming a nice bubbling head. Serve with a straw and a long spoon.

YIELD: 1 10-ounce serving.

THE VCR PARTY

Pop enough light, crunchy corn to fill a tub and drench it in *real* butter. Set out platters of crisp vegetable munchies and lots of smooth, nippy dip. Tuck bowls of salted nuts into every niche. Then dim the houselights and let that classic movie roll.

The VCR party is the "open call" of get-togethers, the kind of easy-going, casual event that makes you want to invite the entire cast of characters who add so much to your life. So throw open the doors! The props should be minimal—just plenty of seating and plump, oversized pillows to fill in the "sprawl space"—and the "staging" nonexistent. Keep your VCR party simple and your friends will focus on the real main feature—those homey good feelings.

Do schedule some intermissions to keep the peanut gallery mixing and mingling—and when you cut to a break, serve up plenty of these palate-pleasers. They'll bring down the house!

The perfect counterpoint to that
classic holiday heartwarmer.

Apple and Spice Lowballer

> 1 cup apple juice
> 3 to 4 apple ice cubes (see
>   page 13)
> ⅛ teaspoon or pinch of ground cinnamon
> 1 lime wedge
> 1 lime slice

Whirl apple juice, apple ice cubes, the cinnamon, and a squirt of lime juice in a blender until the ice is pulverized. Pour into a rocks glass and serve with a straw. Garnish with a lime slice. (For a variation, fill a tall glass ⅔ full and top with well-chilled seltzer water.)

YIELD: 1 8-ounce serving.

SERVE WITH: Oatmeal and raisin bars.

*Marathoning the Brideshead series? Try this
"break special"—long on flavor
and refreshment.*

Kiwi and Ginger Sparkle

1 ripe kiwi fruit, pared and cut up
1 ripe peach, pared, cut up, and pitted
¼ cup crushed ice
Ginger ale, well chilled
2 kiwi slices

Blend the kiwi, peach, and ice in a blender until liquefied, at least 1 minute. Half-fill 2 tall glasses. Fill with ginger ale. Garnish each with a slice of kiwi.

YIELD: 2 10-ounce servings.

SERVE WITH: Soft, ripened Brie and crusty Italian bread.

Hot Tomato with Two Fennel Accents

¼ teaspoon whole fennel seed
1 cup tomato juice
½ teaspoon grated onion
Lemon wedge
Dash of white pepper
Fresh fennel rib, including flavorful bulb
  and fernlike top

In a small saucepan, heat the fennel seed over low heat, pressing with the back of a spoon to release the flavor, until aromatic (about 60 seconds). Add the tomato juice and onion; heat to boiling. Add a squirt of lemon juice and the pepper. Pour into a mug. Garnish with a fennel rib swizzle stick.

YIELD: 1 8-ounce serving.

SERVE WITH: A platter of cheese-topped nachos, fresh from the oven.

Orange Spice Milk Tea

1 cup milk
5 or 6 pieces orange zest (½ by 1 inch),
   cut from 1 orange
2 teaspoons sugar
2 whole allspice
2 whole cloves
1 cinnamon stick
2 cups very hot, freshly brewed tea (see
   How to Brew a Pot of Tea, page 91)
Freshly grated nutmeg

In a small saucepan, heat the milk, 2 pieces of orange zest, sugar, allspice, cloves, and cinnamon stick slowly over low heat. Cover and simmer for 5 minutes.

Meanwhile, brew the tea in a teapot. Strain the milk into the teapot. Pour into 3 cups. Garnish each cup with a strip of orange zest twisted to release the flavor and a grating of nutmeg.

YIELD: 3 cups.

SERVE WITH: Individual walnut tarts or chocolate-covered orange peel.

Vanilla Cappuccino

1 cup milk
½ whole vanilla bean, split
2 teaspoons packed light brown sugar
   (optional)
1½ cups (12 ounces) strong, brewed
   espresso coffee
Ground cinnamon

In a small saucepan, combine the milk and vanilla. Scald the milk. Remove from the heat. Cover and let the milk steep for 5 minutes.

If you like your coffee sweetened, stir sugar into the milk. Reheat the milk briefly over high heat until steaming. Remove the vanilla bean.

Transfer the milk to a blender. Whirl milk until frothy, at least 45 seconds. Half-fill 2 warmed coffee mugs or cups with hot coffee. Add the hot milk, dividing it evenly. Sprinkle the cinnamon lightly on top.

YIELD: 2 cups.

SERVE WITH: Anisette toast or cannoli.

SATURDAY SUMMER LUNCHEON

Gather your friends for a leisurely summer luncheon and you will feast on freshness! Supermarkets, farm stands, green groceries—all are heaped with vine-ripened vegetables that just burst with flavor. Seasonal fruits—peaches, plums, strawberries, raspberries, melons—are at their most colorful, fragrant, and succulent. Capitalize on this beautiful bounty by taking the time to shop for the freshest, firmest produce available, then plan your luncheon menu around the pick of the crop. No recipe, no matter how unique or how well balanced, can compare to the natural goodness of simple whole foods picked at the peak of ripeness.

Then take your celebration al fresco, setting a pretty table in the shade of a tree or under a festive oversized umbrella. If you're a flower gardener, arrange your choicest blooms as a centerpiece, then echo the impact of the flowers by choosing table linens of a similar shade.

Keep the menu as light and airy as the day and you'll have time to enjoy nature's work—and these dazzling luncheon refreshers—to the fullest.

*Hot spices are known to be the best coolers.
The horseradish in this splashy, red refresher
gives an immediate kick, while the pepper
builds its fire more slowly. Cooling cucumber
serves as a balance.*

Tomato and Horseradish Quencher

8 ounces tomato juice
1 tablespoon lemon juice
1 teaspoon horseradish (freshly grated, if
    available), or to taste
Ice cubes
Freshly ground black pepper
Lemon zest (1½ by ½-inch piece)
Cucumber spear, pared and sliced

Stir the tomato juice, lemon juice, and horseradish together in a rocks glass. Add an ice cube
or two.* Top with a grinding of black pepper. Twist
the lemon zest in your fingers to release the flavorful oils and add to the glass. Garnish with a cucumber spear.

YIELD: 1 8-ounce serving.

SERVE WITH: A snappy Cheddar cheese soufflé or
deviled eggs.

* Use tomato juice ice cubes in place of plain ice, if preferred
(see page 78).

For real tang and real flavor,
go back to the source.

Real Cranberry Juice

12-ounce bag (3 cups) cranberries
1 quart water
⅔ cup sugar or to taste
Ice cubes
Orange zest strip (½ by 1½ inches)
   for each serving

Combine the cranberries and water in a saucepan. Heat to boiling; when the berries begin to pop, cover and simmer over low heat for 10 minutes. Strain into a bowl through a fine sieve or a sieve lined with a double thickness of dampened cheesecloth. Press on the pulp with the back of a large spoon.

Stir the sugar into the hot juice until dissolved. Cool at room temperature. Pour into ice-filled tall glasses. Twist a piece of zest to extract the flavorful oils and add to each glass.

This classic good taste is conducive to any celebration.

YIELD: about 4 10-ounce servings, or 1 quart.

SERVE WITH: A bowl of tangerines in the winter; fresh-picked juicy apples in the fall; a bowl of strawberries in the summer; and slices of ripe papaya in the spring. For lunch, serve with a turkey or chicken BLT.

*An everyday staple made just a little special
by the addition of orange juice and
zingy lemon ice.*

Orange and Lemon Spritzer

3 or 4 lemon ice cubes (see
   page 123)
½ cup orange juice, preferably freshly
   squeezed
4 to 6 ounces seltzer water, well chilled
1 slice fresh lemon

Place the ice in a tall glass. Add the orange
juice; then stir in seltzer to fill. Garnish with a
lemon slice.

YIELD: 1 12-ounce serving.

SERVE WITH: A fresh fruit salad topped with a dollop
of yogurt.

The best iced coffee, bar none.

Almond Iced Coffee

1 cup strong brewed coffee
1 cup milk
½ teaspoon vanilla extract
¼ teaspoon almond extract
1 teaspoon sugar (optional)
Ice cubes
Pinch of ground cinnamon

Combine the coffee, milk, extracts, and sugar, if desired. Pour over ice in a tall glass. Sprinkle lightly with ground cinnamon.

YIELD: 2 servings.

SERVE WITH: Westphalian ham and Brie on a croissant.

OCTOBERFEST

Autumn—the season whose first cool blasts of wind blow the last vestiges of summer out of the valleys, chase the tourists away from the seashores, and speed the birds on their long commute to the South. There is no place on earth that does not pause just before the frost is on the pumpkin to raise a glass to a harvest safely put by and to enjoy the crisp, tangy fruits of the season.

Octoberfest is a rousing, rollicking reaffirmation that it is great to be alive—a low-tension, high-spirited breather before the holiday whirl. Celebrate that lingering Indian summer by taking your party outside, where the last charcoals of the barbecue season still scent the air. Be sure to load that well-worn grill with traditional Octoberfest favorites—sizzling bratwurst and spicy, fresh German and Polish sausage.

And whether your celebration has a country-western kick or a hearty Bavarian beat, don't be surprised when the singing begins. There is something about a celebration held on the cusp of winter that compels even the most staid revelers to make some joyful noise. Just provide some hefty mugs of high-sobriety cheer for friends to swing in time to the music and your Octoberfest may not end until November!

*For a party that
will never cool off, try this.*

Chili Pepper-Spiked Hot Tomato Juice

1 cup tomato juice
½ cup chicken broth
½ teaspoon chili powder
Dash of hot pepper sauce, to taste
1 pickled chili pepper

Combine the tomato juice, broth, and chili powder in a small saucepan. Heat to boiling. Add the hot pepper sauce and the chili pepper. Remove from the heat and steep for 5 minutes. Pour into a mug. The pickled chili pepper will float on top.

YIELD: 1 10-ounce serving.

SERVE WITH: Cheddar cheese-topped skillet corn bread or cold shrimp in the shell.

A teaming of two autumn classics—apple and cranberry—with a spicy twist.

Hot Spiced Real Cranberry and Apple Tea

12-ounce bag (3 cups) cranberries
1 quart unsweetened apple juice
⅓ to ½ cup sugar
5 whole cardamom seeds
Zest of ½ orange cut in a long spiral

Combine the cranberries and apple juice in a saucepan. Heat to boiling; when berries begin to pop, cover and simmer over low heat for 10 minutes. Strain into a bowl through a fine sieve or a sieve lined with a double thickness of dampened cheesecloth. (Press the pulp with the back of a spoon.)

Add the sugar gradually, starting with ⅓ cup and tasting to see if you need more. (The natural sweetness of the apple juice is a factor here.) Return to the saucepan; add the cardamom and orange zest. Heat slowly to a boil; cover and steep for 10 minutes. Ladle into mugs.

YIELD: 5 8-ounce servings, or about 5 cups.

SERVE WITH: Slices of cranberry-nut quick bread or other fruited quick breads or muffins.

Clove-Scented Hot Apple and Lemon "Tea"

1 quart water
1 quart apple juice
5 lemons
6 whole cloves
¼ cup packed light brown sugar

Heat the water and apple juice in a large saucepan to boiling. Meanwhile squeeze the juice from 4 lemons (about 1 cup) and cut the remaining lemon into 6 slices. Stick the white pith of each slice with a whole clove.

Stir the lemon juice and the brown sugar together. Off the heat, stir the lemon juice mixture into the hot apple mixture; add the lemon slices. Cover and let stand for 10 minutes.

Ladle into mugs.

YIELD: 8 8-ounce servings, or 2 quarts.

SERVE WITH: Warm, sweet corn muffins, pecan apple muffins, and dried-fruit bar cookies.

When a visit to the farmers' market (or health food store) yields a jug of fresh pear cider, celebrate your good luck with this mulled treat.

Hot Ginger Pear Cider

1 quart pear cider
2 tablespoons minced candied
    ginger slices

Heat the pear cider in a saucepan until simmering. Add the minced ginger. Cover and steep for 5 minutes.

Ladle into mugs, making sure to scrape the bottom of the saucepan so that a few pieces of the ginger find their way into each serving.

YIELD: 4 8-ounce servings, or 1 quart.

SERVE WITH: Crisp gingersnaps or, for real decadence, gingerbread topped with warm lemon sauce or whipped cream.

TREE-TRIMMING PARTY

A Holiday Open-House

Sweep the snow from the welcome mat and throw open the doors! Focus your holiday festivities on trimming that beautiful spruce you've brought in from the cold, and guests won't be able to resist rallying around to light up the occasion.

Pop enough corn to string *and* munch while the creative revelers set to work. Keep fingerfoods within easy reach. For an added touch of cheer, surround your alcohol-free wassail bowl with glowing candles in graduated sizes.

And then, as the last of your cherished ornaments is hung on the tree, lift your glass to the holiday season—and to those friends who make all the occasions of your life so much brighter.

Hot Mulled Apple Cider with Clove-Studded Quince

1 quince *
5 whole cloves
1 gallon fresh apple cider
1 cinnamon stick
A grating of nutmeg

Rub the fuzz from the quince with a damp paper towel. Remove the skin with a paring knife. Stick the cloves into the flesh of the quince.

Place the quince, cider, cinnamon stick, and nutmeg into a large pot. Cover and heat very slowly until simmering (at least 1 hour to allow flavors to blend). Ladle into mugs.

YIELD: 16 8-ounce servings.

SERVE WITH: Thin-sliced smoked ham on warm biscuits; apple, celery, and walnut salad; and pecan tarts or pie for dessert.

* Quince, available in the late fall, adds a blossom-sweet aroma and at the same time a citrusy tang.

Rich Eggnog with Orange and Nutmeg

3 large eggs, separated
½ cup vanilla sugar (see page 53)
3 cups milk
1 cup heavy cream
½ teaspoon grated orange zest
1 teaspoon rum-flavored extract, or to taste
Pinch of salt
Long thin strands of orange zest
Whole nutmeg
Nutmeg grater

In a small bowl, beat the egg yolks and ¼ cup of sugar until light in color and fluffy.

Scald the milk and heavy cream in a medium saucepan. Whisk the scalded milk into the beaten egg. Pour back into the saucepan. Cook, stirring constantly, over low heat until the mixture lightly coats the back of a spoon. (Do not boil or mixture will curdle.) Cool at room temperature, stirring frequently. Add the orange zest and rum extract. Refrigerate until cold.

Just before serving, beat egg whites in a small bowl with the salt until soft peaks form. Gradually beat in the remaining ¼ cup of sugar until stiff peaks form. Fold into the cooled custard.

Pour into chilled punch bowl. Sprinkle the top with strands of orange zest. Ladle into cups and let guests grate some nutmeg onto their eggnog.

YIELD: 12 4-ounce servings, or 1½ quarts.

SERVE WITH: Thin slices of fruitcake, sugared pecans, and thin spiced ginger cookies.

Cranberry/Cherry Punch Bowl

    1 quart cranberry juice, well chilled
    1 pint cherry cider, well chilled
    ½ cup orange juice
    1 orange, thinly sliced
    1 bottle (1 liter/33.8 fluid ounces) seltzer,
      well chilled
    Ice ring (see page 14)

Combine the cranberry juice, cherry cider, orange juice, and orange slices in a large bowl. Stir to blend. Add the seltzer water. Serve in a bowl chilled by an ice wreath thick with green and purple grapes and thin orange slices twisted to look like flowers.

YIELD: about 14 6-ounce servings.

SERVE WITH: Sliced ham and/or turkey, roasted vegetables, corn pudding, potatoes au gratin, and whatever else your heart desires. This punch is savory enough to serve with savory foods.

*This energizer will inspire
any tree-trimmers to reach for the heights!*

Apricot and Almond Punch

2 12-ounce cans apricot nectar, well
    chilled
¼ cup lemon juice
¼ teaspoon almond extract
¼ teaspoon ground cinnamon
1 bottle (1 liter/33.8 fluid ounces) seltzer
    water, well chilled
Ice ring (see page 14)

In a large bowl, combine the apricot nectar,
lemon juice, almond extract, and cinnamon. Stir to
blend. Add the seltzer water. Keep cool with an ice
ring.

YIELD: 10 6-ounce servings.

SERVE WITH: Almond cookies, pound cake, or dried
fruit tarts.

One More Round

Don't stop now! Every new day brings a new reason to celebrate. Promotions, anniversaries, birthdays (especially those that come with lots and lots of candles!) are just a few of the many pleasurable opportunities you'll get to lift your glass in between rousing holiday festivities.

Make those especially intimate occasions events to remember by mixing up original sparkling, spirited, alcohol-free libations that are every bit as unique and personal as your reasons to celebrate. Toast that special birthday with a drink designed to please the guest of honor (whether it's a kicky tonic or a soothing toddy); blend a potent aperitif compatible with that romantic dinner à deux; even mix up a powerful "pick-me-up for one" based on your own favorite taste sensations.

CREATING YOUR OWN DRINKS: THE FLAVOR PRINCIPLE

Is there a mixologist's secret to creating a smooth, satisfying, high-sobriety refresher? You bet there is—but it's really just a question of balance.

Every recipe, whether we are aware of it or not, is a balancing act, a careful melding of certain basic principles at work. (And when these elements come together successfully, our taste buds know it!)

Every satisfying *drink* recipe is a blend of at least two

of the following flavor components: a basic flavor, a neutral flavor, and a balance flavor.

The *basic flavor* can be either sweet/acid or acid/sweet.

The *neutral flavor* is usually an extender such as mineral water or seltzer and can be flavorless, but it can also be a neutrally flavored extender such as ginger ale or one of the essence-flavored waters (such as orange, lemon, or lime sparkling water). The type of extender used—or whether an extender should be used at all—depends on the depth of the basic flavor.

The *balance flavor* is usually a counterpoint or compatible accent flavor to enhance or offset the basic flavor. If the basic flavor is very acid, then the balance flavor will have to be sweet. Conversely, if the basic flavor is sweet, that taste will have to be balanced with an acid.

Confusing? On the following pages we analyze some of the drink recipes in this book. A quick look should help you sort out the basic components.

Coco Colada

Basic flavor: pineapple chunks and juice
 (ACID/sweet)
Neutral flavor: water/seltzer
Balance flavor: cream of coconut
 (SWEET/fat)

The pineapple juice is mostly acid with some sweetness. The seltzer or water extends the flavors so they aren't too concentrated and intense. The cream of coconut adds sweetness to balance the acid of the pineapple and some vegetable fat to add texture as well as flavor.

*Here's another example, this time based
on a savory drink.*

Tomato and Orange Cooler
with Fresh Basil

Basic flavor: tomato juice (ACID)
Neutral flavor: none
Balance flavor: orange juice (SWEET/acid)
**Counterpoints: orange essence and
    fresh basil**

The tomato juice is acid and assertive. There is no neutral flavor. The orange juice balances the acid in the tomato juice.

The orange and tomato juices blend rather well, almost too well, which is why the orange zest, twisted to release the natural oils, acts to reinforce the orange flavor of the juice. The basil adds an interesting bite, providing enough of a counterpoint to keep this combination interesting.

Here's a very simple example.

Real Ginger Ale

Basic flavor: ginger syrup (SWEET/hot)
Neutral flavor: seltzer water
Balance flavor: lime juice (ACID)

The sweetness of the ginger syrup is extended by the seltzer water and sharpened by the acid from the lime.

Ready to start mixing your own? Just begin with the flavor you've been craving, then balance it. Let your taste buds be your guide—and enjoy!

ONE FOR THE ROAD:
ORDERING FROM THE BAR

When your celebration takes you to a well-stocked alcoholic bar, you can still raise a convivial cup and wake up clear-headed tomorrow. You can expect the bartender to have some of these alcohol-free pleasers on hand.

Basic Flavors	Neutral Flavors	Balance Flavors
orange juice	ginger ale	lime wedge
tomato juice	seltzer	lemon wedge
pineapple juice	sparkling water	pickled onion
cranberry juice	club soda	olive
bananas	crushed ice	
fresh strawberries	tonic water	
or strawberries		
in syrup		

Combine them as imaginatively as you would at home, or choose from these well-balanced blends:
- Orange juice, sparkling water, and a lime wedge.
- Tomato juice, tonic water, and an orange twist.
- Tomato juice, orange juice, and an orange twist.
- Pineapple juice, banana, and crushed ice, blended.
- Orange juice, banana, and crushed ice, blended.
- Tomato juice on the rocks with an orange twist.
- Strawberries blended with crushed ice and extended with ginger ale or seltzer water.

NOTE: If sweetened berries are used, add a lime or lemon squirt.

All of the above are very simple examples of basic flavor components at work. The sweet must be balanced with an acid. And if the basic flavor is very assertive, it can be extended with a relatively neutral flavor.

Tools, Helpers, and Hardware

THE BASICS

While definitely low-tech, these very basic hand tools are efficient additions to any home bar:

bar spoon (long handled)
citrus juicer
citrus knife
egg beater (or whisk)
ice crusher (hand operated) *
lemon/lime reamer

mortar and pestle (great for bruising zests and herbs)
fine strainer (or sieve)
shaker (at least 16 ounce)
zester (or sharp vegetable peeler)

THE CONVENIENCES

These appliances can make for faster, easier bartending —and best of all, many are already de rigueur in most kitchens.

Ice Crushers

Electric ice crushers are a definite plus, especially when preparing cool drinks for a crowd. However, they

---

* These are small stainless-steel tools which use leverage to crush about ½ cup of ice at a time. You can crush ice almost as easily by placing cubes in a plastic bag and pummeling with a kitchen mallet or rolling pin.

can be noisy enough to stop party conversations in mid-sentence. When you know you will need a supply of crushed ice, do the work ahead of time (when loud, grinding noises matter least), then store, sealed in a plastic bag, in the freezer.

Blenders

Blenders are the all-purpose bartender's boon. These relatively compact (and quite inexpensive) appliances puree, mix, liquefy, and even crush ice (in drinks) with ease. (And they whip up a mean milkshake!) Choose a variable or multi-speed blender to take full advantage of the appliance's versatility and you'll be turning out creamy potables as well as icy slushes in no time. Especially handy for mixing up smaller batches, the blender is a "must" bar tool. (A plus: most blender jars were made for easy pouring, designed with a lip to keep countertop messes to a minimum.)

Food Processors

While somewhat more costly than the blender, a food processor is capable of performing many culinary tasks. This appliance can crush ice, grate vegetables into more texturey chunks, and slice fruits and vegetables for garnishes, but specifically for drink-making, it is most effective for pureeing and for mixing large batches. The larger capacity processor bowl (about 7 cups) affords you the luxury of producing crowd-sized batches of your favorite drinks, though the pouring can be awkward (and often splashy).

Juicers

Some fruits, happily, need little coaxing to release their juices. Citrus needs only a well-placed prod with a reamer (whether hand-powered or electric), and berries, including grapes and cherries, need to be heated to release their juices. (See our recipe for Real Cranberry

Juice, page 136.) But for drier fruits and vegetables (carrots, apples, pears, etc.) the serious juice-aholic relies upon an extractor to provide flavorful, vitamin-packed straight juices and blends that are as fresh as the fruit or vegetable itself.

Extractors

The extractor is the purist's dream, separating the nutrient-rich liquids from the fruit or vegetable pulp without using heat, a known vitamin and mineral thief. Instead, the machine first pulverizes the flesh of the produce, then extracts the juice by means of centrifugal force. (The liquids strain through a mesh basket while solids and fibrous residue remain trapped there.) The result? An unprocessed juice more akin to the taste of the whole fruit or vegetable, just bursting with vitamins and minerals.

Because good juicers (particularly those available in health food stores) often require a substantial cash outlay, it is not a purchase that can be recommended to consumers who won't be using the appliance with some regularity. However, for those who value fresh flavor and nutritional impact in the juices they drink, even an expensive juicer might seem to be a bargain. (NOTE: Because these fresh juices are not processed, they must be used immediately. They are extremely perishable, and some, like apple juice, can begin to ferment if not consumed at once or frozen.)

Index of Recipes
by Title

Index of Recipes
by Main Ingredients